Ecclesiology
and Ethics

Ecclesiology and Ethics

Ecumenical Ethical Engagement, Moral Formation and the Nature of the Church

Thomas F. Best and Martin Robra, editors

WCC Publications, Geneva

Cover design: Edwin Hassink

ISBN 2-8254-1216-3

© 1997 WCC Publications, World Council of Churches,
150 route de Ferney, 1211 Geneva 2, Switzerland

Printed in Switzerland

Contents

Introduction

Imagine a mighty river waiting to be bridged. On each side are foundations, already built, strong and secure, but different in materials, construction and appearance — and necessarily so, as the landscape and geological formations are different on the two sides of the river. Many doubt that a bridge can be built: the gap is too wide, the foundations may give way! Some argue that it would be too costly to build. Some on both sides would rather that it not be built, preferring not to encourage contact with the other side. Others insist that it *must* be built, arguing that much will be learned in the process, and that anyway there is crucial work to be done, work that can be done only by the two sides together.

The study process

This book brings together the results from the 1992-96 World Council of Churches study on ecclesiology and ethics, a study conducted jointly by Faith and Order (Unit I) and Unit III (Justice, Peace and Creation). In basic terms, it sought to explore the link between what the church *is* and what the church *does*. It explored the ethical dimension not as a separate "department" of the church's life, but as integrally related to its worship, its confession of faith, its witness and service in the world. It explored how the churches practise "moral formation", or training in ethical decision-making and discernment, through their teaching and church life. By linking the nature and unity of the church with the churches' common calling to ethical reflection and action, it aimed to heal divisions between the movements of Faith and Order and Life and Work. And, perhaps most audacious of all, it tried to integrate distinct languages and discourses, especially those of theology and ecclesiology on the one hand, and contemporary Christian ethical reflection on the other.

This book continues the study process by encouraging wide reflection on and discussion of its themes, perspectives and results. Included are the reports — "Costly Unity", "Costly Commitment" and "Costly Obedience" — from the three consultations in the process (at Rønde, Denmark, in 1993; Tantur, near Jerusalem in Israel, in 1994; and Johannesburg, South Africa, in 1996), together with four concise interpretative essays responding to the study, and pointing towards further work, from diverse confessional and cultural points of view.

Thus this book is different from its predecessors, *Costly Unity*[1] and *Costly Commitment*,[2] which included both the papers and report from the Rønde and Tantur meetings respectively. This difference is in response to calls for a "study volume" gathering together the three reports in order to encourage reflection on the study process and its results as a whole, and identifying perspectives and issues for further work. (The papers from the final, Johannesburg, consultation, which were as stimulating and important for that discussion as those of the previous meetings, are published in the July 1997 *Ecumenical Review*.[3] Already published in an earlier issue of the *Review* is the substantial background paper[4] which served as the starting point for the discussion in Johannesburg.)

The details of the study process and its consultations have been given elsewhere and need not be repeated here.[5] The genesis of the study and its place, both within the WCC and the wider ecumenical movement, during these years — from its inception at the combined WCC unit commission meetings at Evian in 1992, through its approval and encouragement by successive WCC central committees, and its evaluation by other WCC bodies, to its final reporting to central committee in 1996 — is an important story in its own right. But that has been told as well.[6] A significant side-effect of the study has been a recovery of portions of the "ecumenical memory" (including some earlier blueprints for bridges!), and that part of the story has perhaps been told best of all.

General perspectives

The study programme has ended, but the study process continues. The reports, of course, carry the "authority" of their own wisdom rather than of WCC commissions or official church bodies. This was necessary, and indeed helpful, for such an exploratory and shorter-term study; but it makes the next stage of the process all the more important. Here the significance of the study will become clearer as Christians and the churches consider its results, test them through their own experience and, we hope, find them to be helpful in their own ecclesiological and ethical reflection and action. To encourage this process of "reception" we provide in this volume, as noted above, four essays examining the study process and its results from diverse perspectives. Most, though not all, of the authors have been involved in the study and all suggest ways in which its concerns can be carried forward.

It is worth noting the striking way in which the *titles* of the three reports have caught the ecumenical imagination. This "litany of 'costlies'", as it has been dubbed, signals a growing awareness of the study's implications and possibilities. The titles reflect a *progression of ecclesiological reflection and deepening of moral concern:* from realizing that "the unity we seek" will turn out — despite our secret hopes? — to be a *costly unity*; through recognizing that "a *costly unity* requires a *costly commitment* to one another"[7] as Christians and as churches; to admitting that it is, finally, not a matter of programmes and institutions, even ecumenical ones, but of a *costly obedience* to our calling to be one and, as one body of Christ, to serve all humanity and creation.

In approaching these reports and interpretative essays, readers should bear in mind the two overarching convictions, or themes, which guided the study as a whole and which provide a framework for reflection on its process and results. The first conviction is that ethical reflection and action — indeed, *ecumenical* ethical reflection and action — are intrinsic to the nature and life of the church. Thus ecclesiological and ethical reflection are inseparable: Christian ethical engagement is an expression of our deepest ecclesiological convictions, and our ecclesiology must be informed by our experience of ethical engagement, by our living out of the gospel in the complex situations of the world. For what we do follows from who we understand ourselves to be, and where we understand ourselves to be at home.

The second conviction is closely related: that ecclesiology and Christian ethics must stay in close dialogue, each honouring and learning from the distinctive language and thought-forms of the other. From the side of ecclesiology this meant the language of koinonia, of hope and memory, eucharist and baptism, of the church. For ethics it involved particularly the notions of the church as "moral community" (one which *necessarily* wrestles, in light of the gospel, with issues of moral import) and of "moral formation", that training in ethical decision-making and discernment which comes through formal church teaching but more pervasively through the whole life of the church, and not least in its worship.[8]

Steps on the way

But if bringing the three reports together in this volume shows a certain inner logic of the study process, it also shows the distinctive character and emphases of its three stages. Readers would do well to approach these reports not as tightly integrated steps in a predetermined "master plan", but rather as successive way-points on a journey whose general direction and goal were known, but whose successive legs could be charted only underway, on the journey itself. By the same token, it is important not to force premature conclusions upon the study, for that would be false to the process itself. Yet we can indicate its principal turning points, the "cairns" or orientation points set by each of the three consultations, and these we wish to review briefly.

The meeting at *Rønde* renewed efforts to relate diverse, too-often separated "wings" of the ecumenical quest as represented in the movements on Faith and Order and Life and Work, taking as an entry point the relation between koinonia and justice, peace and the integrity of creation (JPIC).[9] Its affirmation that "the church not only has, but is, a social ethic, a koinonia ethic"[10] laid the groundwork for the study by insisting that ethical reflection be done also within the theological and ecclesiological "circle", and by naming the ethical dimension as a datum of ecclesiology. The meeting took up some "unfinished business" from the JPIC process, bringing ecclesiological reflections to bear on the notions of "covenant" and "conciliarity", which had been approached within the JPIC process mainly through ethical categories.[11] Rønde reopened the question of the "ecclesial significance" of groups working for justice, peace and the integrity of creation.[12] And it introduced into the ecclesiological discussion the idea — already common coinage in ethical reflection — of the church as "moral community".[13]

Tantur focussed on the ecclesiological significance of ethical reflection and action, while seeing the ethical dimension in relation to the whole life of the church. It was aware of the discussion of Rønde at the fifth world conference on Faith and Order[14] at Santiago de Compostela, and of other reactions, especially to the description of the church as "moral community". Tantur dared to name not just ethical reflection and action, but *ecumenical* ethical reflection and action, as intrinsic to the church.[15] It brought the theme of "covenant" creatively into relation with both eucharist and ethical engagement.[16] Tackling again the relation of issue-oriented groups and movements to the church, Tantur suggested that the term "koinonia" is best used in relation to those linking themselves with the memory and message of Jesus Christ.[17] But Tantur also recognized the "important sense of community"[18] generated within groups whose motivation is not Christian, suggesting that this, "though not ecclesial, may have implications for the way in which we understand church in so far as such communities embody prophetic signs of the reign of God...".[19] Finally, Tantur developed the discussion of church as moral community by exploring one particular way in which the church expresses this identity, namely in the practice of "moral formation". As noted above, this is that process of Christian training in discernment and ethical decision-making which happens not only through formal instruction but through the whole life of the church, including its worship.[20]

Johannesburg focussed on moral formation as a dimension of the ecclesial life of the church, exploring this also within the wider context of the ecumenical movement. It sounded a prophetic note: the world, through its systems and structures, is relentlessly "instructing" us in its values and imposing its priorities upon us; therefore the recovery and strengthening of Christian identity is a key task for Christian moral formation today.[21] Johannesburg thus named the danger of *mal*formation[22] — from which also the church, as human institution, is not immune. Johannesburg also continued the earlier emphasis on worship, focussing on baptism and the eucharist as contexts of formation.[23] A final section[24] experimented with the notion of the ecumenical movement itself as a "moral community", a community "formed" as the gospel "resonates" across the divisions of confession, space and time, a community whose flourishing koinonia is marked both by its growing agreement in matters of faith and church life, and by its common ethical commitments.

It was impossible, of course, to realize all our hopes for the study. In particular the theme of creation was not sufficiently developed, though Johannesburg, as if to acknowledge the problem, ends with a nod in this direction.[25]

Looking ahead

We began by speaking of building bridges. But in introducing the three consultations we have spoken of a journey, of "cairns" and orientation points. This is to change the metaphor and thus to pose, in conclusion, a tantalizing question: what was the real enterprise of the ecclesiology and ethics study? Was it bridge-building — or rather scouting, pathfinding, laying down some points of reference for those who will follow?

Once underway we found ourselves reading not blueprints but half-finished and indistinct maps, with the territory in front of us largely uncharted. Having started as engineers, we ended as scouts, as pathfinders. Those from different sides of the river met in new places. We learned to travel together. We were well supported by those who had sent us — even though, as other scouts and not a few missionaries have found, our reports were not always received comfortably at home! Together we charted both banks of the river afresh, each learning more about the foundation already built on the other side of the river, and on our own. Together we learned what kind of bridge should be built — and how *costly* it will be.

And so we offer these results from the ecclesiology and ethics study with the hope that the bridge-builders who will come after us may find them helpful in their work.

THOMAS F. BEST AND MARTIN ROBRA

NOTES

[1] *Costly Unity: Koinonia and Justice, Peace and Creation*, Thomas F. Best and Wesley Granberg-Michaelson eds, Geneva, WCC, Faith and Order/Unit I and Unit III, 1993.

[2] *Costly Commitment: Ecclesiology and Ethics*, Thomas F. Best and Martin Robra eds, Geneva, Faith and Order/Unit I and Unit III, WCC, 1995. The Tantur papers are also published in *The Ecumenical Review*, vol. 47, no. 2, April 1995, pp.127-87.

[3] See vol. 49, no. 3. An altered version of one of the papers will be published elsewhere. See "The Present Status of the Ecumenical Movement" by Anna Marie Aagaard in the publication of the Tantur Institute's 25th anniversary conference, *The Present Status of Church Unity and Prospects for the Future*, ed. Lawrence Cunningham, Notre Dame, Indiana, Notre Dame UP, forthcoming.

[4] Lewis S. Mudge, "Ecclesiology and Ethics in Current Debate", vol. 48, no. 1, pp.11-27.

[5] See *Costly Unity, op. cit.*, editors' introduction, pp.v-viii; and *Costly Commitment op. cit.*, introduction, pp.vii-x.

[6] *Ibid.*

⁷ See p.28 of this volume, para. 17.

⁸ The ecclesiology and ethics study has helped stimulate fresh work on the relation of worship to ethics. See (from the Tantur consultation) Duncan B. Forrester, "Ecclesiology and Ethics: A Reformed Perspective", in *Costly Commitment, op. cit.*, pp.21-27; also in *The Ecumenical Review*, vol. 47, no. 2, April 1995, pp.148-54; (from Johannesburg) Vigen Guroian, "Moral Formation and Christian Worship", and Duncan B. Forrester, "Moral Formation and Christian Worship", in *The Ecumenical Review*, vol. 49, no. 3, July 1997. From the Faith and Order study programme on worship in relation to the unity of the church see (from the Ditchingham, England, consultation) *So We Believe, So We Pray: Towards Koinonia in Worship*, Thomas F. Best and Dagmar Heller eds, Faith and Order paper no. 171, Geneva, WCC Publications, 1995; (from the Faverges, France, consultation) Vigen Guroian, "On Baptism and the Spirit: The Ethical Significance of the Marks of the Church", and the consultation report, "Become a Christian: The Ethical Implications of Our Common Baptism", publication forthcoming.

⁹ See pp.2-4 of this volume, paras 1-4, quoting Faith and Order texts *Church and World*, the Santiago preparatory text, and *Baptism, Eucharist and Ministry* as well as the "Ten Affirmations" from the JPIC Seoul meeting (para. 3).

¹⁰ See pp.4-5 of this volume, para. 6.

¹¹ See pp.11-13 of this volume, "The concept of covenant", paras 25-30, and "Conciliar fellowship", paras 31-34.

¹² See pp.15-16 of this volume, "II. Koinonia and its implications: Relationships with movements and groups", paras 42-46.

¹³ Ironically this phrase — the occasion for much, sometimes misguided, later comment — was used only twice in the report: once in the text and once in a sub-heading. See para. 1, p.2 of this volume, and sub-head "I. JPIC and the church as moral community".

¹⁴ See *On the Way to Fuller Koinonia: Official Report of the Fifth World Conference on Faith and Order, Santiago de Compostela, 1993*, Thomas F. Best and Günther Gassmann eds, Faith and Order paper no. 166, Geneva, WCC Publications, 1994, report of section I, para. 32, p.235, and report of section IV, paras 30 and 38, pp.259-60 and 261-62.

¹⁵ See pp.28-29 of this volume, para. 17.

¹⁶ See pp.36-39 of this volume, section IV, "Eucharist, covenant and ethical engagement", paras 43-50.

¹⁷ See pp.33-36 of this volume, section III, "The question of 'koinonia-generating involvement'", paras 35-42 and para. 39. Paragraph 35 introduces the topic by referring to Santiago's phrase "koinonia-generating involvement": see *On the Way to Fuller Koinonia, op. cit.*, report of section IV, para. 32, p.260.

¹⁸ See p.36 of this volume, para. 42a.

¹⁹ See p.36 of this volume, para. 42b.

²⁰ See pp.39-48 of this volume, section V, "The ethical character of the *ecclesia:* reflections on moral formation and discernment", paras 51-74.

²¹ See pp.58-61 of this volume, paras 26-29 and 30-35.

²² See pp.61-63 and 68 of this volume, paras 36-42 and 57.

²³ See pp.66-71 of this volume, paras 51-67.

²⁴ See pp.72-87 of this volume, paras 68-116.

²⁵ See p.87 of this volume, para. 116.

Part I

Reports from the
Study Process

Costly Unity

Rønde, Denmark, February 1993

INTRODUCTION

1. The ecumenical movement suffers damage so long as it is unable to bring the justice, peace and the integrity of creation process (JPIC) and the unity discussion into fruitful interaction. The unity movement has, from its very beginnings, wrestled with issues of ecumenical social witness and action. All understandings of the church have affirmed its nature and vocation as a "moral" community. More recently, the conciliar process of mutual commitment to justice, peace and the integrity of creation has brought fresh life and energy to the ecumenical scene. Many claim that JPIC has undeniable ecclesial dimensions and that this conciliar process has been among their most profound experiences of "church".

2. Nonetheless, the cleft between ecumenical forces committed to visible church unity and those focussed on witness, service and moral struggle goes deep and exposes a history of differences which runs the length of the modern ecumenical movement. We may well be convinced that unity and moral conviction are two sides of the same coin but we have not yet given that sufficient and satisfactory expression, and further incantations about the search for unity and the search for justice as inseparable do not really help. The compelling task, then, is serious dialogue about long-lived tensions and divisions. This is the reason we have gathered in Rønde, Denmark, 24-28 February 1993.

3. More common ground exists than many have noted. The essential interconnectedness of the search for the visible unity of the church and the quest for justice, peace and caring for creation has been recently and vigorously underscored. The study document of Faith and Order, *Church and World: The Unity of the Church and the*

Renewal of Human Community (Faith and Order paper no. 151, Geneva, WCC, 1990), has developed those aspects of the Faith and Order tradition which lend themselves precisely to that interaction. More recently, the proposed revision of the working document for the Santiago Faith and Order world conference summarized this stance.

> The church as koinonia is called to share not only in the suffering of its own community but in the suffering of all; by advocacy and care for the poor, needy and marginalized; by joining in all efforts for justice and peace within human societies; by exercising and promoting responsible stewardship of creation and keeping alive hope in the heart of humanity. In so doing it shows its vocation to invite all people to respond in faith to God's love. *Diakonia* to the whole world and koinonia cannot be separated. [1]

The same Faith and Order paper continues:

> We have learned in the process of this work [Faith and Order, Life and Work, and the International Missionary Council] that all realizations of visible unity between churches entail the renewal of broken relationships between members of the church as well as work for renewal, justice and peace in the world (para. 2, p.25).

The eucharistic vision of the church in *Baptism, Eucharist and Ministry* includes the following:

> The eucharist embraces all aspects of life. It is a representative act of thanksgiving and offering on behalf of the whole world. The eucharistic celebration demands reconciliation and sharing among all those regarded as brothers and sisters in the one family of God and is a constant challenge in the search for appropriate relationship in social, economic and political life (Matt. 5:23f.; 1 Cor. 10:16f.; 1 Cor. 11:20-22; Gal. 3:28). All kinds of injustice, racism, separation and lack of freedom are radically challenged when we share in the body and blood of Christ (para. 20).

Likewise, and from the other direction, the justice, peace, and the integrity of creation process gave explicit theological-ethical articulation to its central affirmations:

> Now is the time when the ecumenical movement needs a greater sense of binding, mutual commitment and solidarity in word and action. It is the promise of God's covenant for our time and our world to which we respond. Thus we affirm:
> — that all exercise of power is accountable to God;
> — God's option for the poor;

— the equal value of all races and peoples;
— that male and female are created in the image of God;
— that truth is at the foundation of a community of free people;
— the peace of Jesus Christ;
— the creation as beloved of God;
— that the earth is the Lord's;
— the dignity and commitment of the younger generation;
— that human rights are given by God."[2]

4. All this is substantial common ground and a rich beginning. But it does not of itself address the divergent viewpoints which have long existed in the ecumenical movement. To carry the conversation forward we offer the discussion of these pages, using the Canberra statement (1991) as our springboard. In "The Unity of the Church as Koinonia: Gift and Calling", church unity itself is identified as:

> a koinonia given and expressed in the common confession of the apostolic faith; a common sacramental life… and a common mission witnessing to the gospel of God's grace to all people and serving the whole of creation (para. 2.1).

I. JPIC AND THE CHURCH AS MORAL COMMUNITY

5. The being *(esse)* of the church is at stake in the justice, peace and integrity of creation process. It is not sufficient to affirm that the moral thrust of JPIC is only *related* to the nature and function of the church. More than this is at issue. It can be described from two directions at once, the experience of JPIC as a conciliar process and the experience of the church's nature itself. Koinonia is an apt term for both. It is, for example, an empirically verifiable observation that commitment to and working for particular moral causes creates community among people. The experience of JPIC again and again has been that people have been gathered into a fellowship which can be described as koinonia. Involvement in these struggles of human community generates this koinonia and often enlightens doctrine. An "ecclesio-genetic" power is at work here, frequently moving participants to rich liturgical expression and raising deep religious questions for them, questions of faith and commitment. The power of the Holy Spirit is present here — this is the testimony.
6. At the same time, faith has always claimed the being of the church as itself a "moral" reality. Faith and discipleship are embodied

in and as a community way of life. The memory of Jesus Christ *(anamnesis)*, formative of the church itself, is a force shaping of moral existence. The Trinity is experienced as an image for human community and the basis for social doctrine and ecclesial reality. Such explication could continue, but need not, since it all comes to the same point: the church not only has, but is, a social ethic, a koinonia ethic.

7. Yet a number of complex qualifications must be made in treating the JPIC process and the church as, at heart, moral realities.

7.1. To participate in a particular moral cause does not necessarily signify entry into or belonging in the church. To claim that all approved moral action by non-members somehow makes them church members ("latent" or "anonymous" Christians) is a form of ecclesiastical imperialism. We affirm, however, the experience of fellowship and shared witness which extends beyond the boundaries of the church.

7.2. The church, it must be said, is not *constituted* by or dependent for its ongoing existence upon the moral activities of its members. Its origins and ongoing life rest in the lavish grace and patience of God. However, moral lapses on the part of the members of the church may and often do threaten the credible witness of the church. At this time the church is called to the kind of resistance to the threats to life which JPIC sought to help accomplish. In any case, it is not too much to say that the holiness of the church means the constant moral struggle of its members.

7.3. Given the ambiguity and complexity of so many concrete moral challenges, it is not to be expected that all the members of a particular church, or all church organizations in a particular region, will arrive at the same moral decision in each particular situation. Christian freedom encompasses sincere and serious differences of moral judgment.

7.4. This observation is not an opening of the door to wholesale moral relativism, however. There are boundaries, and it will always be the case that certain decisions and actions are in contradiction to the nature and purpose of the church and the central teaching of the gospel. Instructive past instances of this are those German Christians who uncritically pledged allegiance to the Nazi state, and those South African churches which supported apartheid. In both cases those concerned excluded themselves from the church of Jesus Christ. They were guilty of what Visser 't Hooft described as "moral heresy". Here the being of the church is at stake. It should be added that heavy caution is in order when the stakes of moral judgment are this high, since the boundary is one which draws the line between true and false church. What is both safe to say and important is that serious moral struggle over life issues is always required of the church by its very nature.

7.5. Not all moral concerns carry equal weight, of course. We believe that the church is now called to respond above all, as JPIC did, to threats to life as a moral imperative. Given its role as God's co-worker in the created order and as the proclaimer of the gospel of salvation, the church is bound by its nature and purpose to act decisively when life itself is threatened by whatever forces — economic, political, military and through damage to the environment. Issues of survival are the most compelling for the church.

7.6. Moral issues and struggle often represent the line between "cheap" unity and "costly" unity. Cheap unity avoids morally contested issues because they would disturb the unity of the church. Costly unity is discovering the churches' unity as a gift of pursuing justice and peace. It is often acquired at a price. Consider the struggle for independence in Namibia or the anti-apartheid campaign in South Africa. Forces tried to play off Roman Catholics against Lutherans, Anglicans against Methodists, and indigenous African churches against historic denominations. Genuine unity was discovered in joint struggle, often breaking new ecumenical ground (witness the Kairos document and its ferment). In other cases costly unity is precisely to transcend loyalty to blood and soil, nation and ethnic or class heritage in the name of the God who is one and whose creation is one. It is the unity of the church accomplished on the way of the cross, paid for by the life of Christ and the lives of the martyrs, whose witness inevitably included moral witness. This is unity which, by God's grace, breaks down dividing walls so that we might be reconciled to God and one another. JPIC as a process has often borne testimony to this costly unity. Its enemy is cheap unity — forgiveness without repentance, baptism without discipleship, life without daily dying and rising in a household of faith (the *oikos*) that is to be the visible sign of God's desire for the whole inhabited earth (the *oikoumene*).

8. These comments about moral struggle and unity made, we go on to say that the threats to life today only intensify gratitude to God for the gift of life itself. All creation bears the stamp of holy things. The church, in its whole bearing, should, as a moral community, help foster a "sacramental" orientation towards life, just as the church

understands itself, its being, its mission and witness on a sacramental and eucharistic basis. There is no better place to begin than with the moral meaning of the sacraments themselves. Baptism, for example, is at the heart of the church insofar as the baptized become the effective witness — martyr — to gospel values in the world. Questions of faith and moral and social questions are inseparable from the act of Christian witness that baptism mandates. Eucharist as a sacrament of communion, to cite a second example, is real food for a scattered people in their moral struggle, to heal the brokenness of human being and community. The church sees both its inner unity and solidarity with others as expressions of sharing the bread of life. The sacraments as person-shaping rites can lead us into sacramental living.

9. From its side the efforts for justice, peace and creation have so very often pointed to the essential place of worship and spirituality in our life together. Community is nurtured, hope is sustained, forgiveness is offered, bread for the journey is shared, new energy is discovered. We find a bridge between ecclesiology and ethics in our experience of worship and the deepening of spirituality.

10. The eschatological dimension of both the unity of the church and of JPIC must be affirmed. While the requirements of each will finally be met in God's time and in God's way, that does not invite passivity on our part. On the contrary, our active participation in the concerns for the unity of the church and for justice, peace and the integrity of creation align us with God's final work of fulfilment, just as that final fulfilment prods us to battle the threats to life and claim life itself as the treasure entrusted to us.

II. KOINONIA AND ITS IMPLICATIONS

11. Koinonia is the term proposed as a description for that unity sought by Faith and Order and the conciliar process of justice, peace and the integrity of creation. It entered ecumenical usage in the bilateral dialogues, where its Greek form proved useful in some contexts as a broadening of the Latin *communio*. Koinonia is used in some bilaterals to describe the goal of "communion" without organic union following the removal of possible doctrinal obstacles.

12. The implications of koinonia unfold in the discussion of several dimensions: the notion of Christian ethics itself, the concepts

of covenant, conciliar fellowship, unity and diversity, the local and the global, and relationships with unofficial movements inside and beyond the church as such.

Koinonia and ethics

13. When in the New Testament koinonia refers to the interaction or sharing of believers within the local Christian community, it must be understood as referring to a concrete community of obedience. There can be no doubt that "following Christ" meant very practical things for the early Christians, matters that often brought them into tension and conflict with the surrounding world. Likewise, the intimate connection we find in the New Testament between baptism and newness of life (Eph. 2:1-10) reminds us that choosing to belong to the community implied conscious moral choices.

14. In the course of history, this original and strong relation between faith and moral life was changed and in some cases also weakened. As the church grew and became more institutionalized, and as it became a factor to be reckoned with in the public accession of imperial power in the western world, Christian obedience tended to become formalized; on the one hand along lines of penitence and on the other hand along the lines of compliance with "public orders". Even in churches where a basic connection between liturgy and life was maintained, the sense of radical obedience found in the New Testament — and in later history exemplified by martyrs and saints — diminished.

15. The need to develop "ethics" as a particular discipline arose in modern times as people were faced with the growing complexity of social life. Ethics became the effort to deal with the moral dimensions of this complexity on the basis of autonomous reason, individual judgment and communication by argument. Christians became aware of the growing cleavage between the substance of their tradition and the "foreign" world, and thus were challenged to match this development of ethics by finding ways of relating gospel and world, faith and life, more explicitly.

16. Christian ethics thus developed in different ways: both in alliance with secular approaches (Christian socialism, Christian liberalism) and in opposition to these, when there was a sharp awareness of the basic difference between allegiance to Jesus Christ and allegiance to some modern ideology. In most cases, however, the emphasis on

the individual was taken for granted. As theologians spoke about the life of "the Christian", personal and social-political responsibilities were distinguished.

17. It was an important development when the ecumenical movement, particularly the ecumenical council on Life and Work, began to institutionalize social ethical reflection as reflection of churches with a responsibility to each other and to the world. This effort, which was fuelled by events like the church struggle in Germany in the 1930s and later by analyses of neo-colonialism, dependence and structures of poverty and injustice, helped many Christians to overcome earlier habits of believing in which a certain distance between faith (as the "real" life of the community) and moral life was maintained, or in which the only connection was found in the observance of a certain personal life-style.

18. Recently, on the basis of these developments, Christians have sought to recover the fundamental relation between ethics and koinonia, between moral life and community, and to seek inspiration on the New Testament witness on this point. One of the valuable insights developed in this context is that the community of disciples rather than the individual Christian is the bearer of the tradition and the form and matrix of the moral life. Christian ethics, in this perspective, becomes the reflection on the life of the community in the context and the perspective on the problems of human life in general.

19. Koininia in relation to ethics does not mean in the first instance that the Christian community designs codes and rules; rather that it is a place where, along with the confession of faith and the celebration of the sacraments, and as an inseparable part of it, the gospel tradition is probed permanently for moral inspiration and insight, and where incessant moral counsel keeps the issues of humanity and world alive in the light of the gospel. As such the community is also essentially a place of comfort and support. For some this might mean a consistent emphasis on non-violence; for others a permanent response to the guilt-and-forgiveness dimension of all human life; for still others an effort to recover a sense of calling and covenant in the experience of individual and social life. In all cases, koinonia implies an offer to all human beings involved in moral struggles and in need of frameworks and perspectives. When the moral life of the Christian community is spoken of as witness, this is an essential aspect of it.

Koinonia and other biblical images for the church

20. The proposed revision of the Santiago working document already contains an extended discussion of koinonia. But supplementary comments are needed.

21. Are the different communions ready to see that communion between them — koinonia — whether in matters of faith or of ethical responsibility, calls for steps towards structures of mutual accountability? The fifth world conference on Faith and Order will ask if the churches can take further steps towards "conciliar communion". At the very least, this phrase means being responsible to one another in witnessing to faith in Jesus Christ, and to the implications of this faith for justice, peace, and the integrity of creation. How long will the communions refuse to be challenged by what unity really requires?

22. We must keep in mind that koinonia is only one of several images for the church in the New Testament. It stands alongside expressions such as "people of God", "body of Christ", and the "temple of the Holy Spirit". Indeed the term "church" *(ekklesia)* itself is an image. Each image for the community formed by the gospel carries with it a particular emphasis and context of meaning. Koinonia's primary reference appears to be to the interaction or sharing of believers within the local Christian community. The use of this term to refer to wider relationships is an extension which needs to be carefully considered.

23. What is the potential of koinonia for this purpose? It is important to see that the term means more than merely sharing as such. It means participation in something held or known in common (Acts 2). There is, for instance, koinonia in God, in the Holy Spirit, in Christ, in the faith, in the body of Christ, in the blood of Christ. This alone suggests wider usage. Paul uses koinonia to describe relations between churches in different cities. The collection he takes up for the church in Jerusalem is itself called a *koinonia*. The New Testament usage here and elsewhere marks an extension of the term from what is familiar and homelike to use for building bridges to other, different, communities in faith. This is a bold theological move, especially when Paul extends the calling of Israel to include the Gentiles. The koinonia of which he speaks refers, then, beyond ethnicity and family to a community which exists on the basis of the gospel. Just so, our understanding of koinonia can expand outward to mean a communion in which we share, in Jesus Christ, a common vision for a newly just,

peaceful and responsible world, despite imperfect communions and still-fractured relationships.

24. When koinonia is understood in this still larger sense, as it is in the JPIC process, we begin to be grasped by the imperatives of unity and catholicity in a new way. With this sense of koinonia, there emerges the possibility of a new ecumenical beginning in which the JPIC and Faith and Order movements can share.

The concept of covenant

25. Part of the content of *koinonia is concretized by covenant*. We are acutely aware of misunderstandings of this term which arose at Seoul. The problem lay in the assumption of some that covenant might only mean a compact or common undertaking among human beings. We intend the word here, however, in its full biblical meaning as a relationship initiated by God: a promise to which God is faithful despite all his peoples' failures and transgressions. Thus a covenant between human beings carries the biblical sense only if it is made before God with the intention of obedience to God's covenantal requirements. To enter into this covenant means we accept the conditions under which God sets us in the midst of creation.

26. Some ecumenical documents have turned the noun "covenant" into a verb, "covenanting". This can leave the impression that, since the grammatical subject of the verb is usually ourselves or other human beings, God's authorship of the covenant is being forgotten. For this reason, some may wish to avoid the verbal form altogether. Where it is used, it must be made clear that the covenant involved is still God's, that the covenanting taking place is before God, and that a mutual acceptance of God's conditions and God's commands as best we understand them is indicated.

27. Covenant is an exceedingly rich biblical notion. It is clear, for example, from God's covenant with Noah, that God cares for all of God's creatures, and indeed that the covenant has to do not only with all living things but with creation itself. In Jeremiah, the punishment of God's people for transgression of the covenant is pictured as creation returning to chaos (Jer. 4:23,26-27). Likewise, the restoration of the community of faith is accompanied by the restoration of the natural environment. Furthermore, the use of the term "covenant" in the New Testament does not annul, but rather fulfils, though not in a supercessionist way, the covenant with Israel. In this context the implications of the covenant for seeking and doing justice become clear.

28. Numerous New Testament references, particularly in Ephesians and Colossians, fill out these meanings, connecting covenant once again to the renewal of creation. The "new covenant in my blood" of the eucharist further binds God's calling of the community of faith to the transformation of the created order. The deepest purpose of the covenant has been made manifest through the incarnation, cross and resurrection of Jesus Christ.

29. A crucial issue raised by the JPIC movement is precisely the question of ecclesiology in relation to creation, redemption and eschatology. The covenant notion offers helpful perspectives, as already noted. Yet we must not allow "covenant" to carry the full weight of what we have to say about gospel, history and creation. There are other grounds for developing this relationship and its implications.

30. However these inquiries may go, it is important to insist that any contemporary reaffirmation of God's covenant with us as God's people have specific content in the same way that ancient Israel's obedience had the content of Torah as interpreted by the teaching of the prophets. In short, the covenant needs to be spelled out in some sort of social creed. We offer as an example of such content the "Criteria for Economic Policy" contained in Part IV of *Christian Faith and the World Economy Today*, produced by Unit III of the World Council of Churches. [3]

Conciliar fellowship

31. Our intention is not to use the theme of koinonia as the sole model for the unity we seek. In particular, this term must not be interpreted as meaning acceptance of our present denominational structures so long as they are "in communion". That would make koinonia only a synonym for "reconciled diversity". We need to look at what the JPIC movement does with the notion of conciliarity. Perhaps it provides a way of returning to this notion (as, for example in the term "conciliar fellowship" adopted at the Nairobi assembly) and giving it a fuller meaning.

32. We note with interest the phraseology of the proposed revision of the working document for Santiago: "... further work of Faith and Order should focus on right structures serving a conciliar communion (cf. Canberra statement, para. 2:1) of churches under the guidance of the Holy Spirit (John 16:13) and an authentic exercise of authority" (p.19, para. 17). In the context of JPIC we can see where such

"conciliar communion" could be of assistance. In the questions both of diversity/unity and locality/universality, conciliar communion could serve as an indispensable frame of reference. Such conciliar communion could be a framework within which divergent views might vigorously engage each other within koinonia. As issues of justice enter the unity debate, we need to ask what models of conciliar communion best promote the church's witness.

33. As noted earlier, ecumenical accountability among the churches is weak. There need to be structures of accountability even before conciliar communion is achieved. May conciliarity in some form be possible even before full communion is established? The JPIC movement has pressed for this in order that we may give a united witness to justice, peace and the integrity of creation. We urge the churches to get into a habit of conciliar accountability, even as we are on the way to a fuller relationship. Of course all efforts to develop such conciliar practice must be fully transparent and above board, or they will not earn the churches' cooperation and respect.

34. As it considers conciliar communion, Faith and Order should look into the very practical matter of ecclesiastical bureaucracy. Complex administrative structures have been added to the life of the churches in this century without giving them ecclesiological meaning. There is danger that these structures will become bureaucratic, in the pejorative sense, precisely because they are not ecclesiologically accountable. In what sense, if at all, is the reality of bureaucracy taken into account in ecclesiology? What is the relation between bureaucracy and the accountability needs of conciliar relationships? Nearly every church today maintains some sort of office to deal with relationships to other churches and to ecumenical bodies. The World Council of Churches itself has moved in a bureaucratic direction. Can koinonia be expressed bureaucratically? Can bureaucracy be the vehicle of the Holy Spirit?

The local and the global

35. We face a complex set of issues regarding local insights and initiatives on the one hand and global issues on the other. In the contemporary world every local issue has its global implications, and every global issue asks for local response. Yet there are often blockages at both ends. Not all JPIC issues have achieved adequate local translations. And local groups of Christians often fail to catch the global reality in which they live.

36. Yet it is too simple to think only of two levels. The "local" means different things in different circumstances. It may mean a neighbourhood, or a nation, or a region of the world. And sometimes an issue may be global in its importance, yet not susceptible of any single explanation or formula so varied are its ramifications in different places. Sometimes a global issue is such that it comes to expression most clearly in some particular locality, whose Christian people then have special responsibility for defining its significance for the rest of the *oikoumene*. Sometimes an essentially local issue can only be clearly seen when its global aspects are grasped. We need new forms of expression for both the local and the global, depending on the issue and the setting in which it can most trenchantly be formulated.

37. In this connection it is important to recall the theme of catholicity as an attribute of the church, together with the developments of this theme at the New Delhi and Nairobi assemblies. At New Delhi we lifted up the local dimension without forgetting the universal, speaking of "all in each place" bound together in "a fully committed fellowship". At Nairobi we lifted up the universal dimension without forgetting the local, speaking of "conciliar fellowship". Together these themes help us envision a universal koinonia of mutual commitment embracing local *oikoumenes* across the globe. The JPIC process has been a formidable instrument for this.

Diversity and unity

38. Diversity has long been an important ecclesial fact and theme. But we sense that the situation has changed. What used to be diversity has now in many places become fragmentation and brokenness. In many places each congregation is virtually unique in its interpretation of the faith. Localism in the church goes beyond "congregationalism" as a polity. The latter is principled and has an understanding of the church universal. What we see today amounts to a resurgence of tribalism, hardly a synonym for the diversity we have claimed and cherished.

39. Differing expressions of the apostolic faith corresponding to different cultural situations have long been known and understood. Already in the early church, the apostolic faith existed in many cultures and languages, with widely differing customs, including liturgical texts and forms. As the New Testament shows, diversity of this sort can indeed lead to conflict. Koinonia in conciliar structures allowed that controversy to be dealt with in love and responsibility. So

it may be today. No one doubts that many different customs, liturgies and theological formulas represent legitimate forms of Christian faith and practice, or that controversy is to be expected and made creative within the fellowship.

40. There is an important difference, however, today. Diversity used to be considered acceptable and containable because there was a universal framework of theological understanding acknowledged by the whole church. Now the universal framework of Christianity itself is under radical attack. In the absence of clarity about what is to be believed "at all times, everywhere, and by all" (Vincent of Lérins) local variety looks quite different and raises questions which cause great difficulty.

41. How can such diverse expressions of the faith be kept in communication with one another? How can one speak of accountability in such situations? These are problems for which at the moment we have no adequate answers. We suspect that one reason for our dilemma is lack of confidence about the nature of our faith at the centre. The many local versions of faith have no clear affirmation of faith at the centre to which to respond.

Relationships with movements and groups

42. There are questions here at two levels. The first involves ecclesial relations with Christian movements which may not feel the sense of accountability that should be present in the established organs of the church. The JPIC perspective makes clear that much of the energy in seeking justice and peace is to be found in groups of this kind. They bear an important witness to official church bodies.

43. In many cases relationships to such movements raise the question of the "laity" in a new form. It is clear that lay groups can do much to move the JPIC and Faith and Order agendas forward, and that in doing so they will often form their own policies and take their own initiatives. The problem is one of authority and representation. If much of the energy on social issues in a church is in the hands of the people, how does the church take account of that fact in its official relationships? We need to see the church as a movement of the people of God, not merely as a structure. We need to say more about the *whole* people of God. We recommend another look at the first paragraphs of the ministry text of *Baptism, Eucharist and Ministry*. This is a classic statement about the whole people that needs to be

remembered. The Santiago document does not say enough about the "people of God" in this larger sense.

44. But there is also the issue of cooperation with people of good will outside the Christian faith whose goals and methods seem similar to ours, and whose knowledge and commitment often exceed what we can muster. These are other "koinonias" having their own structures, relationships and priorities.

45. We must not underestimate the theological importance of these relationships with people of other faiths or no faith. Many of us who despair about the church's commitment to JPIC issues find better koinonia in collaborating with people outside. This is no mere theoretical problem. It is an existential problem for growing numbers of Christians today who sense that on some issues — environmental degradation for example — there may not be time to wait for the churches in their official structures to respond.

46. How are we to look at such relationships? It is still our own faith, our vision of the gospel, that guides us as we reach out to others. We may try to see the church as a sounding board, or as a medium of expression, for movements rooted outside it. For many people the church can call attention to what is going on in the world. At the same time, it is possible in the light of Jesus Christ to look at forms of caring koinonia outside the church as movements of the Holy Spirit gathering people to serve God in ways they may not fully understand. In humility, the church may seek to point to what the Spirit is doing outside its visible boundaries, as well as within, thus witnessing to the wider work of God in the world of creation.

III. DIFFERENT ANALYSES AND RESPONSES

47. There are many overall assessments of the direction history is going. Each sketches the story being enacted in our world in a different way and each affects the churches' response. For some, the predominant trend is the triumph of democratic capitalism. Trends in Eastern Europe and the former Soviet Union, despite setbacks, are interpreted to mean that one side "won the cold war", with incalculable benefits to humankind. For others, the salient trend is towards one form or another of communitarianism. The "civil society" of peoples' participation, mutual responsibility and initiative over against the state is seen in motion everywhere and as the promise of

the future. Still others feel that, however important such trends may be, they are overwhelmed by evidence of the degradation of the human condition. Starvation, pollution, ethnic cleansing, political oppression, the AIDS epidemic: these tell the true story, and our only course is to resist and do what we can; most ominous of all, the life support systems of the planet are being slowly shut down and the great struggle for survival begins. Yet another school claims that global technologization and its economic accompaniments have rendered irrelevant all great ideas and struggles. There will be no more crusades and no more drama: we will simply be managed by instruments of our own creation. History as turbulent and creative human drama is at an end. Finally, there are those who see nothing new at all. Passing events are simply rearrangements of perennial plagues and sins: scarcity, human pride, the lust for power, wealth and glory.

48. Our response is forged from what we see around us and the clues we choose to interpret the whole. They shape the church itself and interact with its basic stances towards the world. Thus we must also take into account the diversity of responses within Christianity. There are at least five: (1) the state of the world means that this is the end of history, that the Second Coming is rapidly approaching, and therefore the primary task is to convert and baptize; (2) the world has always been this way, the poor will be always with us, there will be wars and rumours of wars — the best response of the churches is contemplative withdrawal and prayer for the world; (3) the church must offer an example of an alternative society that models itself on the values of the kingdom of God; (4) in light of the situation in the world, the church needs to take a leading role, even giving direction to initiatives for justice and peace; and (5) the church has to enter into the struggles of the people, not leading the process but sharing in it.

49. In different measures, all these approaches are present in our churches. The problem is not with the diversity, but with our use of various approaches for competitive or defensive purposes and with the paralysis this creates both in our response to injustice and broken community, and for genuine dialogue with one another.

50. Within the ecumenical movement, and the WCC specifically, different analyses have been set forth to undergird the Christian concern for social justice, and to indicate a common vision of society which the churches could share and promote. These specific perspectives remained open for further debate and evolved in the course of the years. In the 1950s, the "responsible society" predominated. In the

1960s, with the rise of the challenge of the third world, the model of development and rapid social change became the emphasis. The 1966 Church and Society world conference examined different social-ethical views of changes, including revolutionary action for justice. In the late 1970s the Just, Participatory and Sustainable Society (JPSS) became prominent, attempting to bring together various approaches (with the theme of "sustainability" making a contribution to emerging global awareness). And in the 1980s Justice, Peace and the Integrity of Creation took centre stage.

51. Often the tendency has been to canonize one position and to reject the others, therefore denying the diversity of analyses or of contexts within which churches have their faith, life and witness. Almost every view is at least partially true. None can claim the whole truth.

52. Nonetheless, even amidst this plurality of perspectives, we do not approach the changing world situation as a *tabula rasa*. In Seoul, we adopted ten affirmations and basic criteria for discernment of the path our moral life should take and sensed a moral centre around which we can all gather. In our ongoing work on ecclesiology and ethics no debate is closed. We are provided a place for serious engagement, making clear that no analysis or action is imposed and no participant is regarded with contempt.

CONCLUSION

53. The ecumenical movement suffers damage so long as it is unable to bring the justice, peace and the integrity of creation process and the unity discussion into fruitful interaction. We have sought in this document to show that such interaction is both possible and promising.

The appendices indicate how this process can now be carried forward in specific ways.

NOTES

[1] "Towards *Koinonia* in Faith, Life and Witness", rev. version, 12 February 1993, para. 17, p.13.
[2] Cf. *Now Is the Time*, JPIC Final Document, Geneva, WCC, 1990, pp.12-20.
[3] Geneva, WCC Publications, 1992.

APPENDIX I
SUGGESTIONS TO FAITH AND ORDER
FOR SANTIAGO DE COMPOSTELA

1. We recognize with gratitude that the Faith and Order commission in its preparation for the Santiago world conference and the process of study after the conference has set out a promising road of reflection in which the concerns alive in the JPIC process are taken seriously. We hope that this paves the way for future cooperation within the WCC that will enhance the effectiveness of the Council in its communication with member churches and others, and thus strengthen the witness of the church in the world.

2. We strongly recommend sharing the report of our consultation with the delegates to the Santiago world conference. We feel that this report strengthens and supplements insights found in the proposed revision of the Santiago working document, "Towards Koinonia in Faith, Life and Witness", and that it can help delegates see how specific Faith and Order concerns might be placed in a wider framework of common ecumenical challenges.

3. We have noticed that the proposed revision of the Santiago working document "Towards Koinonia in Faith, Life, and Witness" is a vast improvement compared with the original version. That is particularly the case for the addition of the section on humanity and creation (I.2) and for many elaborations in the text which emphasize the moral dimension of the Christian life. There remain, however, points at which we have hesitancies or would suggest different wording:

3.1. As to page 1, paragraph 1, we would generally welcome more serious attention to the divergence that can be observed among the various ways of interpreting the world situation, and especially to the way that divergence affects the unity of the ecumenical response. It is a source of concern for us that we are no longer on solid common ground in this respect, and that the chaotic world situation tends to strengthen disagreement and division, and consequently uncertainty and anxiety in the relations among the churches.

3.2. We feel that the Canberra statement on unity does not yet deserve the status of "classic ecumenical text", but that it needs further work. We suggest that the Santiago conference devote a part of its energies to just this work.

3.3. We would appreciate more serious attention to the fact that the implementation of the call to unity requires different methods and emphases in different parts of the world. Interchurch dialogue may not be the only or most appropriate instrument everywhere. The issue of non-theological factors takes on particular relevance here.

3.4. We note that the document contains no reference to the dialogue with Judaism. We are convinced, however, that any document that deals with "covenant" should include a consideration of the bond with the Jewish people.

3.5. We wonder whether the term "ethical living" (IV.2) is an improvement over "discipleship".

APPENDIX II
SUGGESTIONS TO THE WORLD COUNCIL OF CHURCHES

1. We are grateful to the WCC for calling this consultation as a joint effort between Unit I and Unit III. We feel that it was timely and necessary. We have made a beginning with a discussion of the fundamental issues involved, but also feel very strongly that it was only a beginning. The process leading eventually to specific forms of integrating previously separated emphases in WCC work needs to be continued, and certain steps have to be taken in order to ensure that it does not come to a standstill. We regard the Faith and Order world conference in Santiago in August 1993, the Unit III Commission meeting in October 1993, and the meeting of the central committee in 1994 in Johannesburg as landmarks that should play a specific role in this regard. We recommend that before too long another consultation be organized to move the discussion further. Above all we would urge a new official impetus to the JPIC programme as a central WCC focus. It would greatly help local churches and groups to receive an unambiguous signal from the WCC on this point. The development of the ten affirmations of Seoul as a kind of ecumenical catechism might be a suitable instrument here.

2. We realize that several issues remain to be considered in the general area of ecclesiology and ethics before anything like a common framework can become visible and convincing. The WCC should continue to consider the ways different traditions express in their ecclesiologies binding and shaping approaches to ethical questions (the liturgy after the liturgy, status confessionis, building the kingdom of God, etc.). This process should, however, be directly linked to local experiences of the interconnectedness of faith and action and

move between an investigation of the moral substance of traditions and the moral experience of the people of God today. Out of this dialogical process the meaning of such key terms as "conciliar process", "covenanting", and "koinonia" can be explored as further linkage of JPIC and the visible unity of the church. Units I and III together have chief responsibility for this. Significant beginnings have already been made, we add, in the overlooked document of the WCC executive committee, Kinshasa 1986, "Initial Hypotheses on the Ecclesiological Dimensions of the Ecumenical Process of Covenanting on Justice, Peace and Integrity of Creation", and in the Faith and Order study document *Church and World: The Unity of the Church and the Renewal of Human Community* (Faith and Order paper no. 151, Geneva, WCC, 1990).

3. In our consultation we have again realized the importance of "ecumenical memory". Beside the presence of people who could bring alive for us the concerns of local contexts, we were greatly helped by the presence of those who had been involved in WCC work, be it in Faith and Order or in Church and Society and JPIC. They saw to it that we would not repeat earlier discussions but could take due note of previous points of debate and consensus. Against this background we want to express our wish that the WCC make an explicit effort to protect and develop such ecumenical memory by consciously creating and sustaining a "community of elders" in the ecumenical movement. Our concern is that sometimes people are invited to participate in the work of the WCC who have no previous experience except perhaps the attendance of one assembly. Therefore, the need for adequate ecumenical formation should be honoured. Nurturing new voices remains critical for the ecumenical future.

4. In relation to the previous point we want to express some serious concern about the use of the "quota system". Obviously, one of the tasks of the WCC is to organize the ecumenical debate in ways which enable full participation and exchange between a range of views. Only in this way can the discussion move forward to new common insights and commitments. The basic purpose of the quota system is to ensure precisely such participation. It is our experience, however, that through legalistic application the system has become self-defeating and that it now narrows rather than ensures constructive exchange. In some cases the expertise required for the debate has been eliminated. We suggest, therefore, that the principle of the quota

system be used with more freedom, and in respect of the needs for a realistic organization of the ecumenical debate.

5. We wish to underline the need for a more conciliar style of working in and among the various offices of the WCC. Our consultation has made us realize to what extent various concerns and programme emphases have grown into separate establishments which tend to defend their vested interests over against each other. Misunderstandings and conflicts between different departments in the WCC form one aspect of this; much more serious, however, is that the separate establishments also institutionalize their relations with local churches and groups in separate ways. This strengthens and sometimes even creates serious divisions within and among churches on the local level. There is an urgent need for the WCC to develop a coherent image. Much internal change seems to be required to achieve this.

6. A more conciliar style will be facilitated by cultivating the art of listening. Participants in dialogue again and again need to translate into their own vocabulary terms that others use rather than attempt to impose their own vocabulary. Similarly we need a basic respect for different starting points — the activist, the academic, the ecclesiastical, for instance. Special mention should be made of expertise, both expert knowledge and analysis which help test our assumptions and perspectives. We also must question forms of meetings and decision-making that have a built-in cultural bias that interferes with full participation or where significant constituencies such as women and youth are under-represented.

7. We also point out that the WCC lacks instruments appropriate to the changed situation for support of local ecumenism and collective global witness. It is essential for a system of dialogue to be in place which enables local ecumenism to challenge the forms of global ecumenism, and nurtures mutual accountability between the two.

List of Participants

Anna Marie Aagaard, Denmark
    (co-moderator)
Agnes Abuom, Kenya
Paul A. Crow, Jr, USA
P. Patelisio Finau, Tonga Islands
James H. Forest, USA
Bonnie Greene, Canada

Bert Hoedemaker, Netherlands
Anton W.J. Houtepen, Netherlands
Margot Kässmann, Germany
José Míguez Bonino, Argentina
    (co-moderator)
Erica Dolly Mphuthi, Lesotho
Lewis S. Mudge, USA

D. Preman Niles, Sri Lanka
Rüdiger Noll, Germany
Jong-Wha Park, Korea
Larry Rasmussen, USA
Neville Richardson, South Africa
Ioan Sauca, Romania
Silvia Regina de Lima Silva, Brazil
Veronica Swai, Tanzania
Louise Tappa, Cameroon
Constance Tarasar, USA
Juan Antonio Vera-Mendez,
   Puerto Rico
Lukas Vischer, Switzerland
Mar Theophilus Zacharias, India

WCC staff

Unit I: Unity and Renewal
Ion Bria, interim unit convenor
Evelyn Appiah, programme assistant,
   Lay Centres desk
Thomas F. Best, executive secretary,
   Faith and Order

Unit III: Justice, Peace and Creation
Jae Shik Oh, interim unit convenor
Wesley Granberg-Michaelson, executive secretary, Economy, Ecology
   and Sustainable Society
Peony Wong, administrative assistant,
   Economy, Ecology and Sustainable Society

Costly Commitment

Tantur Ecumenical Institute, Israel, November 1994

PREFACE

1. This report — a record of work in progress — develops material produced at a meeting on the relation of ecclesiology and ethics held at the Tantur Ecumenical Institute, Jerusalem, in November 1994. This gathering was the second in a series organized by the World Council of Churches Unit III (Justice, Peace and Creation) and Faith and Order (Unit I/Unity and Renewal). The first consultation, held at Rønde, Denmark, in February 1993, [1] explored issues of koinonia in relation to justice, peace and the integrity of creation. A third consultation will focus on the role of moral formation within the life of the churches, in relation both to their search for visible unity and to their witness in the world.

2. We record here our warm thanks to Father Thomas Stransky and to the whole staff of Tantur for their hospitality and generous support. We wish them God's blessings and all success in their mission of justice, reconciliation and peace within the troubled context of the city of Jerusalem and of the Middle East.

I. INTRODUCTION: THE RELATION OF ECCLESIOLOGY AND ETHICS

3. In and through the ecumenical movement the churches have learned to reflect and act together. Together they have confessed that though we live in the reality of the world we live *from* the reality of God, who made the situation of humankind and the wider creation his own in order to redeem and transform it. Together they have brought

hope through the gospel message and witnessed to that coming kingdom which is God's promise and goal for the whole of creation.

4. Yet their continuing divisions on important matters of faith, order, life and work have often prevented the churches from offering a unified witness on crucial ethical issues. These divisions among the churches reveal the brokenness of their koinonia, and hamper their prophetic mission and service in the world.

5. Some historical reminders will serve to sharpen this point. In the 1930s the ecumenical movement was unable to bring the churches of Europe to unite in opposition to rearmament. During the German church struggle against Nazism, the ecumenical movement found it exceedingly difficult to give its unequivocal support to the Confessing Church for fear of destroying its fragile relationship with the Evangelical Church in Germany as a whole.

6. After the second world war, the establishment of the World Council of Churches in 1948 signalled the resolve of the ecumenical community both to work for the fuller unity of the church and to participate in the struggle for a new just world order. Already in 1952 the third world conference on Faith and Order at Lund had issued the following challenge:

> Should not our churches... act together in all matters except those in which deep differences of conviction compel them to act separately?[2]

Since then there have been continuing efforts within the ecumenical movement to foster the churches' common witness and action, and to relate these to the search for visible unity.

7. A notable expression of the churches' resolve to "act together" was the establishment of the WCC's Programme to Combat Racism (PCR) during the 1970s. But even then, some WCC member churches questioned the ecclesiological legitimacy of this programme. Some tried to hamper its work by arguing that it might disrupt the work of Faith and Order in its quest for the unity of the church — a view which Faith and Order explicitly rejected in the statement "Towards Unity in Tension".[3]

8. The need to relate ecclesiology and ethics, while long recognized within the ecumenical movement, has assumed a special urgency in recent years and has become a leading theme in recent ecumenical work. This is reflected in the meetings and texts to which we have referred in our reflections at Tantur (thus the Faith and Order/ JPIC consultation at Rønde [*Costly Unity*[4]]; the Faith and Order study

document *Church and World;*[5] the fifth world conference on Faith and Order held at Santiago de Compostela, Spain, in August 1993;[6] and the seventh assembly of the World Council of Churches in Canberra.[7]

9. This urgency is felt, in part, because of the complexity and severity of the challenges confronting humanity and the wider creation today. The background document for the fifth world conference on Faith and Order ("Towards Koinonia in Faith, Life and Witness"[8]) made strong mention of new and unsettling world situations that challenge the Christian churches to witness to Jesus Christ in ways perhaps not yet even conceived. To take examples from the social and political sphere, at Tantur we recalled how in the past decade geopolitical hegemonies, especially in eastern Europe and the former Soviet Union, have collapsed; initially these developments had raised possibilities for peace, but were soon revealed as deeply threatening to fragile human communities which were left naked and without the moral resources to combat brutal and violent uses of power. As the same document noted, "we are witnesses of national disintegration and also of conflicting nationalistic tendencies".[9] Problems have arisen not only for nations struggling to establish peace with neigh-bours, but also for societies seeking to build up their "moral fibre" where the churches have been repressed for decades. Similar problems face both church and society in the Middle East, in the Balkans and in the Caucasus. And in Western Europe and North America the moral influence of the churches has seriously diminished, resulting in a breakdown of those values necessary for a healthy and dynamic "civil society".

10. It is in full awareness of such situations that we have explored the relationship between ecclesiology and ethics. This relationship is not merely an abstract or theoretical matter; here we touch issues of life and death, of deep conviction and commitment. Here we deal with a fundamental *vocation* of the church and of Christians who work together in facing crucial issues of today. Thus we affirm wholeheart-edly the call made by the churches at the WCC seventh assembly in Canberra in 1991

> to recommit themselves to work for justice, peace and the integrity of creation, linking more closely the search for sacramental communion of the church with the struggles for justice and peace.[10]

Furthermore, the churches must commit themselves to one another, recognizing that they need each other on the ecumenical journey. Such commitment is an essential foundation for their common reflection and action. It becomes increasingly clear that the road to a *costly unity* leads necessarily through a *costly commitment* of the churches to one another.

11. Such a commitment has sustained the fellowship of the ecumenical movement, even when it has been placed under considerable strain by such issues as mentioned above. This commitment is expressed, on the one hand, in a growing consensus on the need to affirm and emphasize the *ethical* character of the church (over against those who were previously wary of "moral reductionism"). As stressed in *Church and World*, this has direct consequences for our understanding of "the unity which we seek":

> The connection between unity and justice makes it necessary to ask of every expression of visible unity: "Does it promote justice in the light of the gospel of Jesus Christ, both within the church and the world?" and secondly, "Does it foster the engagement of the church in God's work for justice?"[11]

12. This commitment is equally expressed, on the other hand, by a concern for *ecclesial* renewal amongst those who have been more deeply engaged in ethical praxis. The situation in South Africa today is particularly indicative of this latter need. Now that the struggle against apartheid as the governing ideology is at an end, the South African Council of Churches and its member churches, who were deeply engaged in that struggle, are being forced to give urgent attention to the recovery of a concern for ecclesial unity and fellowship in the task of national reconstruction, the development of a moral society and a just democratic culture. (One sign of unity and renewal in this situation is the formation in April 1994 of the Uniting Reformed Church in Southern Africa. But far more remains to be done to manifest fully the unifying power of the gospel against the forces of hatred, fear and division.)

13. Another side of the issue is seen in the strong identification of the Armenian Orthodox Church with the Armenian people in the present conflict with Azerbaijan over the fate of Nagorno-Karabagh. In many other cases too the historical form of ecclesiastical institutions comes into tension with the evangelical mission of the church, and the preaching of a gospel that transcends ethnic particularism and eschews violence.

II. BASIC CONVICTIONS

14. At Tantur we found ourselves in agreement on certain basic convictions which undergird our efforts to inter-relate ecclesiology and ethics. These perspectives, which are recorded briefly below, concern the ecumenical dimension of our work, the nature of the ecumenical journey, issues of grace and discipleship, the distinctive resources for Christian engagement in ethical issues, and the relation of Christian ethics to ethical reflection as practised within society generally.

A. The ecumenical dimension is fundamental

15. At Tantur we faced with special urgency a series of questions arising from our conviction that unity and ethical engagement, ecclesiology and ethics, belong together. We listened to the experience of Christians working together for peace, for justice and for the care of creation. We were mindful of the fact that we were meeting in Jerusalem — that "city of peace" dreamt of by the prophets of so many generations, a city defined by the intersection of so many strands of history and tradition and so in need of healing. From all these factors we have become especially aware of the *ecumenical* dimension of our topic.

16. Despite all the complexities described in paragraphs 5-13 above, the ecumenical struggles of recent decades have had significant results. They have left important moral "deposits": the reverence for the dignity of all persons as creatures of God, the affirmation of the fundamental equality of women and men, the "option for the poor", the rejection of racial barriers, a strong "no" to nuclear armaments, the pursuit of non-violent strategies for conflict resolution, and the imperative for a responsible stewardship of the environment — all these are *ecumenical* achievements, given by God as the churches have worked together on crucial ethical issues facing humanity and creation.

17. We believe that the churches have not yet grasped the full implications of this decisive "ecumenical dimension". The churches have not fully realized that a *costly unity* requires a *costly commitment* to one another. We believe that the experience of the churches in facing ethical issues together poses fundamental ecclesiological questions, not only to the ecumenical movement but also to the churches themselves. Thus we invite Christians and the churches to join us in considering the following questions:

a) What difference does it make that the churches increasingly reflect — and act — *together* in responding to ethical issues?

b) Is there an *ecclesial* dimension to the reality of Christians coming together across the lines of confession and tradition and, through their common service, "being Christ for the other" (Martin Luther) in that place?

c) Is it enough to say (as we did in *Church and World* and *Costly Unity*) that ethical engagement is intrinsic to the church *as* church? Is it enough to say that, if a church is not engaging responsibly with the ethical issues of its day, it is not being fully church? Must we not also say: if the churches are not engaging these ethical issues *together*, then *none of them individually is being fully church*?

B. The ecumenical journey

18. In our reflections on these questions we began from the affirmation of the fifth world conference on Faith and Order that:

> The church is the community of people called by God who, through the Holy Spirit, are united with Jesus Christ and sent as his disciples to witness to and participate in God's reconciliation, healing and transformation of creation. [12]

At Tantur we explored again the meaning of this vocation of the church within the trinitarian work of reconciliation, healing and transformation. Our experience of ecumenical reflection and engagement, and the history of the ecumenical movement in both its success and failure, offer us encouragement and challenge for our future work. This experience and this history have led us to see that the quest for unity and the struggle for justice are integral to the life of the church. They should not be separated.

19. So, too, we have been led to see that the fullness of the church is more manifest when this integral vision is embraced by the churches *together* rather than separately. The koinonia which Christians and the churches increasingly share is itself a source of inspiration — and challenge — for their further work on issues of ecclesiology and ethics.

20. Yet with the WCC Canberra assembly we acknowledge that, despite such significant examples of common reflection and action as given in paragraph 16 above, often the

> churches have failed to draw the consequences for their life from the degree of communion they have already experienced and the agreements already achieved. [13]

Thus the churches are still challenged by the affirmation made at Lund in 1952, and referred to in paragraph 6 above: that common reflection and action, common confession, mission, witness and service should be the *norm*, rather than the exception, in the lives of the churches today.

C. The church: grace and discipleship

21. The church is God's gracious gift to us; this grace calls forth and shapes the moral life of disciples. We rely on God's forgiveness and renewing grace in our faithfulness and infidelity, in our virtue and our sin. The church does not rest on moral achievement, but on justification, on God's justice and not our own. It is on this basis that we affirm that moral engagement, common action and reflection are intrinsic to the very life and being of the church. Thus we affirm the original intention of *Costly Unity*, paragraph 7.2, to say that while the church is not constituted by or dependent for its ongoing existence upon the moral activities of its members, the holiness of the church calls for their constant moral struggle.

22. In the living Christian community there can be no ecclesiology without ethics and no ethics without ecclesiology. As Santiago de Compostela reminds us,

> The being and mission of the church, therefore, are at stake in witness through proclamation and concrete actions for justice, peace and integrity of creation. This is a defining mark of koinonia and central to our understanding of ecclesiology... our theological reflection on the proper unity of Christ's church is inevitably related to ethics. [14]

23. The traditional marks of the church — oneness, catholicity, apostolicity and holiness — are all to be expressed in the moral life of its members. Oneness calls for deepening love and communion; catholicity involves a welcome to rich diversity within community; apostolicity suggests reaching out to the neighbour in sharing truth received from Jesus Christ; and straightforward, unselfconscious goodness is an essential dimension of holiness. These are central expressions of what it means to be the body of Christ.

24. The discipline of discipleship, which is both corporate and personal, involves witness to the truth and loving service. God's loving discipline is a sign that we are God's children; it is "for our good, that we may share his holiness" (Heb. 12:10); it is training in discipleship *(paideia)*, which is for our encouragement:

Therefore lift your drooping hands and strengthen your weak knees, and make straight paths for your feet, so that what is lame may not be put out of joint but rather be healed (Heb. 12:12).

This is reflected in the structures of discipline in the churches, which provide for nurture (formation), pastoral care, and the integrity of the community, and frequently are concerned also with the institutions of society, with doing justice in social life, and with the healing of broken relationships.

25. A process of discernment is proper to the Christian community as koinonia, and is an essential part of its life. As *Costly Unity* affirms, the Christian community is

> a place where, along with the confession of faith and the celebration of the sacraments, and as an inseparable part of it, the gospel tradition is probed permanently for moral inspiration and insight, and where incessant moral counsel keeps the issues of humanity and world alive in light of the gospel. [15]

26. Thus as disciples we are called together to a constant process of discernment how best to participate, in the light of our faith, in the moral struggles, complexities and challenges facing humankind. This discerning of the signs of the times is a constant responsibility for Christians and the church (Matt. 16:1-4). It is only to the faithful and the humble that it is given to discover the signs of the coming of God's reign in the midst of the confusions of the world's history, and to adjust their behaviour to this discernment of God's purpose and call. Disciples are not left to face these tasks alone; they are equipped with formidable resources in the form of their hope for God's future for humanity and creation, and their memory of God's gracious gifts given in past and present.

D. Hope and memory: resources for Christian engagement

27. "In the kingdom of God both the church and the whole of humanity have their goal." [16] The church looks forward to the kingdom with hope. While the church through its own striving does not bring about the rule of God, the church's life as a witnessing and serving community is part of its coming.

> The kingdom is a gift; its full realization is the very work of God. As partakers of the trinitarian life, however, the members of the church are called to be co-workers with God (1 Cor. 3:9) for the implementation of the values of the kingdom in the world. [17]

28. The ethical reflection and engagement of the church, as it wrestles with the moral issues and problems of today, takes place at an intersection of future, past and present. Its account of the moral life, expressed in its commitment to specific actions in response to particular situations of need, is shaped in a threefold interaction, the elements of which are (a) its hope for the realization of God's promises for humanity and creation; (b) the sources of its life in scripture and Tradition, worship and reflection; and (c) all the complexities of the issues confronting the church and Christians today. In shaping and putting into practice its response to the issues of the day it is enlivened by its hope for the coming kingdom, the disturbing memory *(anamnesis)* of Jesus Christ, and the sanctifying and renewing power of the Spirit.

29. In this process the church looks not only to itself and its own life; it is called to be in solidarity with the whole of creation, and its witness and service is given in the name of Christ, in whom the whole creation has its purpose and goal.

30. The fullness of God's purpose for humanity and creation (Rom. 8:15-39; Col. 1:15-29; Eph. 1:3-10) is a constant judgment upon our partial and imperfect response to the issues confronting us today. But our hope for the kingdom, and our experience of God's forgiveness and mercy, empower us to continue our witness and service in the world.

E. Ethics, church and humankind

31. Ethics is a general human enterprise: to be human is to be a moral agent. Reflection on the human condition and its relation to nature has taken various forms throughout history. There has always been a complex interrelation between Christian ethics and various other ethical approaches. Therefore, reflection on the relation of ethics and ecclesiology necessarily includes reflection on the ways in which modern culture affects the societies and the cultures to which the church belongs.

32. For its part, Christian ethics relates both to the church and to the wider creation. It is rooted in and shaped by the eucharistic community, and as such it does not stand aloof from the moral struggles of humankind. Christian ethics can define itself fully only in relation to both the eucharistic community and to the wider creation, on the basis of the nature of the church itself. As *Baptism, Eucharist and Ministry* emphasizes,

The eucharist embraces all aspects of life. It is representative act of thanksgiving and offering on behalf of the whole world. The eucharistic celebration demands reconciliation and sharing among all those regarded as brothers and sisters in the one family of God and is a constant challenge in the search for appropriate relationships in social, economic and political life (Matt. 5:23f.; 1 Cor. 10:16f.; 1 Cor. 11:20-22; Gal. 3:28). All kinds of injustice, racism, separation and lack of freedom are radically challenged when were shared in the body and blood of Christ. [18]

33. This leads to a series of questions about the relation of Christian ethics to other forms of secular and religious ethics. How does the church relate to this public realm? How does Christian ethics relate to the ways in which human beings face moral issues? What are its methods in putting these issues into the perspective of the kingdom? How does Christian ethics relate to the various ethical theories important in ethical reflection today? More generally, how does Christian ethics relate to the various ways of life, and their moral underpinnings?

34. These issues require sustained attention from the churches and the ecumenical movement. They are not only practical but missiological and therefore fundamentally theological in nature. They invite us to speak theologically about humankind and creation, its unity and destiny, the ambiguities of its struggles. These ambiguities, too, belong to the life of the church. The integrity and relevance of the churches' social witness and moral life depend on the degree to which they are taken seriously.

III. THE QUESTION OF "KOINONIA-GENERATING INVOLVEMENT"

35. We also considered the complex and sensitive issue of what the fifth world conference on Faith and Order called "koinonia-generating involvement". This refers to the possible ecclesial significance of experiences (both within and outside the traditional boundaries of the church) of community arising through work for justice, peace or the stewardship of creation. Thus Santiago de Compostela stated:

We affirm that, in many places and at different levels, koinonia-generating involvement in the struggles of humanity is taking place. We recognize in these common involvements an urgent, real, but imperfect koinonia, and urge the Faith and Order commission to give priority to lifting up and clarifying their ecclesiological implications. [19]

36. It is helpful to set this issue within a larger context. The quest for fuller koinonia among churches and their members is an essential aspect of the ecclesial and ethical dynamic among those engaged in the ecumenical movement. This applies to churches with long traditions, to churches which have emerged from processes of theological and institutional reformation, to churches which have been integrated for centuries in a given culture, to churches springing (whether in the 4th or the 19th century C.E.) from the missionary efforts of other churches, and to the so-called "new" or "independent" churches. It also applies to experiences of koinonia arising in and through common engagement, within and across the lines of the various Christian traditions and confessions, for human dignity and justice, peace, or the safeguarding of creation. All these expressions of the Christian tradition are equally called to find ways to discover and enliven koinonia within themselves and amongst one another.

37. But these are not the only experiences of shared participation and, in the view of some, of koinonia. *Costly Unity* pointed to two other contexts in which common engagement in ethical issues may raise ecclesiologically significant questions. One has to do with the sense of participation and commitment experienced in "Christian movements which may not feel the sense of accountability that should be present in the established organs of the church". *Costly Unity* noted that these groups "bear an important witness to official church bodies". [20] There is a profound experience of church stemming from communities of the faithful who dare to become involved in particular issues, and find that their experience challenges the traditional ways of living and probing the gospel. Examples would include some Christian "base communities" in Latin America; prayer groups, movements and action groups identifying themselves as Christian but not in direct contact with official structures of the churches; and groups of women who claim a Christian identity yet, due to their experience, feel that the church is distant or alienated from them.

38. A second area is "the issue of cooperation with people of good will outside the Christian faith". [21] This points to another experience, one beyond the confines of the church, in which persons who do not claim to be Christians (and sometimes openly refuse to be identified with them, or with the church) may share with Christians specific

moral goals and actions. Some would use the term "koinonia" also for such wider experiences, to point to that sense of community arising from common reflection and engagement on ethical issues of today. Surely we are called to celebrate such a sense of community, and to affirm the efforts of all persons of goodwill on behalf of humanity and the creation.

39. Nevertheless because the term "koinonia" is rooted in the New Testament, and has a long and particular history in theological and ecclesiological discussion, there are advantages in reserving it for use in specifically Christian contexts. It is best used in reference to the church or to Christian groups, whether those related directly to the church or those whose relation to the church is more distant, but who claim a clear Christian motivation for their work. This is intended to affirm that Christians bring to their engagement in ethical issues the distinctive resources of their faith, their tradition, and their life in Christian community. It is not meant to judge, or lessen the importance of, the community formed among those outside the church as they work together on issues of justice. Indeed by clarifying such distinctions one can better appreciate that community on its own terms.

40. Because the Spirit is constantly renewing the church and the world, we should expect new things, new experiences of faith, new expressions of the church coming to life. In this spirit we are called to face a changing world. It is changing first of all due to the work of Christ, both within and outside of the church. And since God has granted humanity the liberty — with all its benefits and dangers — to participate in the preservation and transformation of the world, human efforts and agency are part of this work. Through Christians and non-Christians, the Spirit is "making all things new".

41. We summarize these reflections in a series of affirmations. These are given here to encourage reflection and discussion among the churches and those engaged in movements of witness and action, both within and outside of the church. The following statements concern the koinonia generated by Christian involvement in ethical issues:

a) Koinonia is generated and nurtured as churches and Christians reflect together on issues of ethical concern, and seek a response to the challenges facing humanity and the creation today.
b) Such koinonia may be experienced both within the church, and among Christian groups not directly related to official church structures.

c) These statements, in turn, raise serious questions for ecumenical reflection:

    1) There is a reality of Christian koinonia not directly connected to official church structures. How does this relate to the renewal which has taken place among followers of Christ over the centuries — a renewal which has, indeed, sometimes meant the emergence of new church bodies?

    2) What are the gifts, and where are the limits, of such developments?

    3) How do we distinguish renewal from fragmentation and disintegration?

42. Other affirmations concern the wider human community and its engagement with the issues of today. Thus we note that:

a) An important sense of community is generated among those who (while not connected with the church and not claiming a Christian motivation) work together on issues facing humanity and creation today.

b) This sense of community, though not ecclesial, may have implications for the way in which we understand church in so far as such communities embody prophetic signs of the reign of God and bring not only the world but also the churches closer to God's mysterious purpose in the world.

IV. EUCHARIST, COVENANT AND ETHICAL ENGAGEMENT

43. Christian traditions have understood the relationship of ecclesiology and ethics in diverse ways. Distinctive perspectives — for example, the "liturgy after the liturgy", the "confessing church", the witness of the historic peace churches — illuminate different, and important, aspects of this relationship. Several such "models" for understanding, and living out, the link between ecclesiology and ethics were explored at the Glion meeting within the JPIC process, and are referred to in *Costly Unity*.[22] This exploration needs to continue, not least because these models for linking ecclesiology and ethics are in many ways convergent. At Tantur we discovered a convergence through the notion of covenant in relation to eucharist, and this is developed in outline form below.

A. Eucharist

44. The eucharist, as *anamnesis* of God's salvific act in Christ, is the starting point for Christian life, witness and transforming service. As foretaste of the fulfilment to come the eucharist is also, in a certain sense, the place where all human endeavours find their completion and are offered to the Father in the paschal mystery of Christ, in order to become in him thanksgiving and doxology.

45. In the eucharist, Christians living in the world and involved in the joys, sufferings and expectations of humankind come together in response to God's call. This coming together has many aspects, among which are the following:

a) The eucharistic assembly is a living image of the church, the church which the Father is calling and gathering around the world.

b) The believers listen together to God's word and are renewed in their discipleship and mission.

c) Partaking in the same body and blood of Christ they are called to a love without limits. They are called to transcend all barriers, in their celebrating community and in the world.

d) In prayer and thanksgiving they are called to become a living and a spiritual offering, not only in worship, but in all their commitments and in their life as a whole.

e) The eucharist is also the meal of the kingdom, a foretaste of God's final fulfilment in store for humanity and creation. As a consequence, Christians are called to live today in tension with the promises of the kingdom in its fullness, the kingdom yet to come.

46. Each of these dimensions of the eucharist implies a true and demanding commitment to witness and service. Surely — as noted in paragraph 32 — "all kinds of injustice, racism, separation and lack of freedom are radically challenged when we share in the body and blood of Christ..."[23]

B. Covenant

47. The covenant, as an expression of God's will for humankind and creation, creates an indestructible relationship between the living church gathered for worship, and the church as it is church in the world. To state this schematically:

a) The covenant in the Old and New Testaments which God offers to humankind in word and sacrament — a covenant expressed according to Christians most clearly in the life, death and resurrection of Jesus Christ — finds a special expression in the celebration of the eucharist. This celebration is itself called "testament" or "koinonia" (1 Cor. 11).

b)   The same term, "koinonia", also describes the ethical engagement of Christians (thus Rom. 15:26 on the collection of money for "the poor" in Jerusalem; this act is not only "a sign" of koinonia, but *is* koinonia).

The conciliar process on justice, peace and the integrity of creation has, with good reason, emphasized the importance of covenant as undergirding the church's ethical actions.

48. This reflection is complemented and deepened when covenant is seen in its intrinsic relation to the eucharist. The link made above between the covenant, in both Old and New Testaments, and the eucharist is made also by *Baptism, Eucharist and Ministry*. At the beginning of its consideration of the eucharist, BEM notes that:

> Christians see the eucharist prefigured in the passover memorial of Israel's deliverance from the land of bondage and in the meal of the covenant on Mount Sinai (Ex. 24). It is the new paschal meal of the church, the meal of the new covenant, which Christ gave to his disciples as the *anamnesis* of his death and resurrection, as the anticipation of the supper of the Lamb (Rev. 19:9). [24]

C. Eucharist and ethical engagement as expressions of koinonia

49. Thus on the basis of the Christian understanding, we may say that the eucharist and ethical engagement are both expressions of God's covenant. Put differently, using the language of our earlier discussion of koinonia, we may speak of a "continuum" between the koinonia given and experienced in the eucharist, and the koinonia given and experienced in ethical engagement. Stated again schematically:

a)   The koinonia experienced in the eucharist and the koinonia experienced in ethical engagement — these two dimensions of the covenant — are, each in their own way, an *anamnesis*. That is, they are an active remembering, a "re-presenting" of the covenant between God, humankind and creation, a testimony to God's mighty acts (1 Pet. 2:12). They make visible to the world God's initiative in Jesus Christ for the salvation of humankind and creation, and God's insistence upon just relationships between human beings, and between human beings and the whole creation.

b)   Both dimensions are filled with the confidence of the certainty of the coming kingdom of God, and are signs and foretastes of this kingdom. They engage the church to be open faithfully for the future.

c) One of their common goals is the realization of life lived in full dignity. This will make persons joyful and thereby also make God joyful.

50. Furthermore, these two experiences of the one koinonia are strongly interdependent: one cannot exist without the other. This is apparent in 1 Corinthians 11:17-22, where Paul criticizes the celebration of the Lord's supper among the Corinthian Christians on the grounds that it treats some members of the community unjustly. This emphasizes that (again stated schematically):

a) Eucharistic koinonia has always an ethical manifestation. If this is not the case, the koinonia is betrayed and degenerates into spiritualism.

b) Ethical koinonia is always grounded in the life of worship (most especially, in the eucharist). If this is not the case, the koinonia is imperfect and degenerates into activism and moralism.

V. THE ETHICAL CHARACTER OF THE EKKLESIA: REFLECTIONS ON MORAL FORMATION AND DISCERNMENT

51. At Tantur we have reaffirmed our conviction that ethics belongs to the *esse* of the church. In spelling out the implications of this for the life of Christians and the church, we have reflected particularly on the notions of moral formation and discernment. As part of this process we have entered into discussion with reactions to *Costly Unity*, and have considered one particular understanding of the church (the "ethos of the household of faith") in more detail as a resource for ethical reflection and engagement.

52. The categories of moral formation and discernment follow from the nature of the church and its life as church in the world. The churches are expected to provide important moral resources both for their own members and for the wider world. This involves, as part of the churches' overall task of spiritual formation, the moral formation of the faithful. An important part of this is training in discernment, helping church members to analyze ethical issues from the perspective of the gospel and preparing them to judge "how best to participate in the light of their faith in the moral struggles, complexities and challenges" of the present day (see para. 26 above). More broadly the

churches are expected to contribute to the moral well-being of the societies in which they live, for example through informed participation in public debate on specific ethical issues. The fraying of the "moral fibre" in many societies makes this role all the more urgent today.

A. Moral formation and moral community

53. The language of "moral formation" clarifies and takes forward the discussion of church as "moral community" which featured at the Rønde consultation. There it was noted that "all understandings of the church have affirmed its nature and vocation as a 'moral' community".[25] This language points to the fact that the church and its members are, necessarily, moral agents whose actions reflect, consciously or unconsciously, their values and convictions. This language has proved helpful in focussing on aspects of the church's life which promote, or hinder, its participation in public discourse, and the shaping of public policy, in secular and pluralistic societies.

54. Within such societies moral discourse, having lost its traditional foundation, is in a state of confusion. Here the church may make an important witness by taking stands on issues of the day, through educational campaigns, through works of mercy, through the ministry of the laity in society, through the quality of its own community life, and so on. To identify the church as a "moral community" makes clear its right — indeed, its responsibility — to participate in such ways in the wider life of society.

55. We recognize that the term "moral community" has engendered considerable debate, not least at Tantur. Difficulties have arisen through the term being *mis*heard as a full description of the ethical character of the ekklesia. Certainly Rønde did not intend any reductionism of the church, leading to moralism or a self-righteous triumphalism. For Rønde the identity of the church as "moral community" is a gift of God, a part, though not the whole, of the fullness of the church. The term "moral" has also been *mis*heard as "moralistic", thus confusing our understanding of the ekklesia with such movements as Moral Rearmament or the "moral majority", or as representing the ethical character of the ekklesia as an individual or "ghetto" morality.

56. At Tantur we explored how the language of "moral formation" and "discernment" can carry forward the discussion of the ethical nature of the church, and its implications for the life of the church in the world. Thus "moral formation" is not understood as an alternative

to "moral community", but as one explication and development of this perspective on the reality of church.

B. Moral formation: A resource for ecumenical reflection

57. Attention to moral formation and discernment is a promising way to explore dimensions of the church's very nature and mission. This approach helps discover the riches, as well as the shortcomings, of the various church traditions in facing ethical issues. The process of moral formation and discernment — and the moral inquiry which belongs to it — can offer a language for the churches to speak both among themselves and to society. Because this process, though it may be carried out differently, is common to both church and world, it offers a helpful bridge from the reality of the church to issues of society's well-being. It is indeed a promising avenue for ecumenical inquiry and ecumenical formation.

58. The process of "moral formation" and discernment within the Christian community means an openness to new realities, insofar as they are consistent with the work of God. Here discernment is not always easy. For example, moral assessment is helpful not least in analyzing patterns of power and power relationships. But power may be used both for good and for evil, and the analysis of situations in the "real world" will often have to grapple with the ambiguity of good and evil in complex ethical decisions.

59. Such "discernment of the spirits" inevitably involves an informed critique of the world's structures and hidden agendas. Thus the process of moral assessment will sometimes call the church, in faith, to sharp prophetic judgment upon society. It will sometimes lead the church to advocate a life-style which is counter to prevailing cultural values (for example, in criticizing a "consumerism" which values material gain and possessions more highly than persons).

60. This process will sometimes call the church to *self*-criticism, reminding it how these same worldly forces and structures affect its own life as an historical institution. Sometimes the church will need to confess that, wittingly or unwittingly, it condones attitudes which allow injustice to continue or which obscure the root causes of injustice. Sometimes the church will discover that its own processes of ethical judgment, and of moral formation, have become distorted by such factors.

61. Moral formation indicates the *shaping* of human character and conduct from a moral point of view; it involves both "being" and

"doing". Moral discernment indicates *how* we decide what we are to be and to do, that is, how character should be nurtured and what decisions and actions we take on particular moral issues. Of course all human interaction plays a role in forming character, and shaping decisions and actions; the process is, in this sense, "worldly", and continual. But this only emphasizes the need for the churches *as churches* to offer both nurture and discriminating judgment.

62. This process takes place within the ethos or environment of a particular society, community or church. The songs we sing, the stories we tell, the issues we debate, the instruction we offer, the persons thought worth emulating, the common habits and practices of a culture — these are the sources and "signatures" of "our" ethos. And the "moral environment" is marked not least by the way a community, society or church is ordered — who does what, by what means, and with what kind of authority. Thus it is the whole *way of life* which morally forms and educates (or malforms and miseducates), and this way of life both creates and reflects a particular moral ethos.

63. The language of moral formation and discernment can be helpful for the ecumenical discussion in several ways. For one, it would "mine" the moral substance of our various understandings and images of church. For example, consider the traditional "marks" of the church as developed in terms of the Christian moral life in paragraph 23 above. The "oneness" of the church, it was there suggested, implies that its members should act so as to deepen their love and communion; the "catholicity" of the church implies behaviour that is welcoming of diversity within community. The language of moral formation and discernment would ask: what kind of environment nurtures such moral practices? What patterns of behaviour help create and foster them? What virtues, values, obligations and moral vision do each of these marks imply for Christian catechesis and the life of the church as a whole? How should church life be ordered to promote these practices? How are these practices a source for spiritual and moral discernment on specific issues which Christians face?

64. The church has, from its heritage, many scriptural and traditional resources for pursuing the moral dimension intrinsic to the life of the church. The questions in paragraph 63 above could be posed in respect of other rich images and understandings of the church, such as the body of Christ, the discipleship community, church as sign and sacrament, the covenant community and so on. For example, what

resources for moral formation and discernment follow from starting from "eucharistic community" as a designation for the life of the church?

65. We discussed one of these "rich images and understandings" in more detail, namely the *ekklesia* understood as a saving, eucharistic and covenantal "household of faith". The term is rooted in scripture and able potentially to describe the ethical character of the church. [26] Such images, however, are not simply abstract ideas for understanding church; they help shape and undergird various ways of living out our faith in the world. This broader dimension we indicate by using the term "ethos". Thus in speaking of the "*ethos* of the household of faith" we mean the way of life, the distinctive patterns of thinking, feeling and acting, which characterize those who live within that "household". (This recalls the etymological and theological connection between "ethos" and "ethics".)

a) We acknowledge that every image or metaphor for the church is inadequate, and unable to illuminate the full range of ecclesiological issues and problems. In particular we acknowledge the patriarchal and hierarchical nature of the Graeco-Roman household; any use of the "household" metaphor must take into account how the early Christian movement transformed some values from its prevailing culture, while accepting others. Yet we still affirm that the "household [Greek *oikos*] of faith" is a productive metaphor for focussing on various dimensions of the ethical character of the church.

b) It points to the local household of faith in each place (in our terms today, to local congregations, to monastic communities, base communities and so on) but also beyond this, to the ecumenical movement, the universal church, and the *oikoumene*. The term is located ecclesiology within the trinitarian economy of salvation and points beyond the present to the eschatological fulfilment of the *oikoumene*.

c) The concept of household *(oikos)* also relates the witness of the church to the economic and ecological realities of our world, in which such realities as the exploitation of creation, and widespread poverty, contradict the message of the reign of God. [27] It points to how the church "in each place" manages its life in relation to its witness in the world. It points equally to the ethical accountability of the universal church, in relation both to the local church and to the global concerns for justice, peace and the integrity of creation. Understood in this way, the notion of *oikos* mediates between the micro and macro levels of human life and activity.

d) Moreover the "ethos of the household of faith" also refers to the social and cultural context within which the moral formation of the members of the church occurs. Here we note especially the connection between the "household of faith" and the various households or families which make up the church and which are fundamental to the moral formation of its members. [28] As St John Chrysostom reminds us, "the household is a little church"; if we regulate it properly, he continues, "we will also be fit to oversee the church". Thus the term encourages us to take account of the family and its special role in creating, nurturing and sustaining the ethical aspect which is intrinsic to the church.

e) One matter of prime importance for the ethos of the household of faith is the relationships among the persons within it, and the way in which they participate together in its life and mission. The Christian ethos implies that relations within the church are intended to be covenantal, to be shaped and nurtured by the gospel and by the liturgy of the church. At their best, such relationships affirm human equality and nurture plurality at all "levels" of the life of the church and of society. This has clear implications for the structure of the church and the relations of power within it. Various churches are structured in different ways; but however the internal life of a particular "household of faith" is organized, a true understanding of *oikos* excludes the suppression of some members of the community by others (as, for example, in a system of patriarchal domination). It encourages the full use of each person's gifts *(charismata)*, and celebrates the variety of cultures and communities found within the one household.

f) Each household of faith must respect and nourish the relationships among its members, lest they become distorted by the misuse of power. When the church fails to fulfil its responsibility in this regard, it contributes to the creation of a moral vacuum in society — a vacuum soon filled by distorted forms of the *oikos*. This is seen today in the emergence of new and often violent national-isms, religious fundamentalisms, and nihilistic forms of secular-ism. These undermine and destroy genuine forms of human community, and are contrary to the character and purpose of the household of faith. Christians need urgently to participate with others in nourishing the values which help to form and sustain just societies which promote the growth and fulfilment of their members. This leads to reflections on the "moral formation" of Christians as a priority within the household of faith.

66. This is an example of how one particular image may enrich our reflection on the ethical dimension of church. It is important to note that each such ecclesial "perspective" will nurture some virtues more than others, prize some values more than others, emphasize some obligations more than others. Each will shape some particular vision of the Christian moral life, bringing the Good, the Beautiful, and the True together in different and distinctive constellations. (Of course, the Christian life carries many images at once: but then the particular combination creates *its* moral ethos.)

C. Moral formation: Its context in the life of the church and the world

67. Such understandings and images must also be understood in their historical, sociological and psychological dimensions, for these contribute to their effect upon persons and communities. Moral formation, too, has its "genes" and this means that the process of formation and discernment must take seriously the *experience* of the church in each place. At issue is how Christian teachings and values have related to wider cultural patterns, and have actually been embodied in daily life. This involves the consideration of what patterns of daily life, what values, virtues, obligations and visions actually developed as the church interacted with the wider society; how what was taught as "the Christian life" was actually put into practice day by day; and what was the concrete moral *substance* of sin, salvation and redemption as experienced in daily life.

68. We take now a concrete example to show the potential of moral inquiry as an ecumenical language for understanding the ethical dimensions of church. This is the relation between moral formation and discernment, and the various ways in which churches of the *oikoumene* are "ordered".

a) Such inquiry assumes that the ordering of a church is already both a creation of, and a reflection on, its ethos and way of life: a polity *is* already an ethic. How gifts (charisms) are ordered, and roles assigned and carried out, is already a way of being people of God together and a way, as church, of being *in* the world. So if the perennial Christian "strategy" is (1) to gather the people, (2) to break the bread, and (3) to tell the stories, then certain questions follow.

b) These questions include the following: What shape does the gathering take? Do some sit in designated seats in carefully arranged spaces while others sit elsewhere? Who breaks the bread? If only some, for what reasons? Who tells the stories? Do the gathered speak in turn, with some speaking first or foremost in accord with some teaching, tradition, or practice? Are some designated "proclaimers of the word" and others "hearers" of it? Do all perhaps take a turn, without regard for status or office? Or are there no "turns" at all, and each speaks as the Spirit prompts in the midst of the congregation? Are some stories "more" stories than others, holding formal or informal canonical status? Are some interpretations and interpreters more authoritative than others? If so, on what grounds?

c) Whatever answers are given, there is a further and more basic level of questions: what are the *reasons for* such differences among Christian communities? what moral ethos and substance belongs to each of them?

The point is that *how* church is ordered has consequences for spiritual and moral formation and discernment, and thus is subject to scrutiny of the kind we propose. Practices, structures and roles (like moral exemplars and like catechesis) are morally potent.

69. There are, of course, reasons other than moral ones for ordering church the way we do — the understanding of scripture, the witness of tradition, historical experience — and these are vital. Yet they do not remove the need for a moral assessment of *how* the church "is" a way of life of its own, and a way of life within the world. For *how* church is manifest as a way of life indicates what it regards as good, right and fitting.

70. Moral assessment is also an important means by which the church can make its presence felt in society. For these same questions can be posed by the churches to the world in which they live, in the interest of fostering the moral formation of the human community (and of exposing its *mal*formation). This is because communities, too, live from explicit and implicit understandings of the good life; they nurture some virtues, values, obligations and visions more than others; they shape, for better and worse, human character and conduct. And the way in which they are ordered and governed in all

arenas of life is morally potent, and subject to assessment and correction.

71. These reflections on moral formation have important implications for our understanding of the church. While affirming the transcendent reality of the church we recognize that the church is not yet, in its empirical historical manifestation, fully what it is in God. In this sense we can say that the church as historic institution is itself undergoing a process of "moral formation" guided by God, a process which will continue until the full reign of God dawns. Thus the tasks of spiritual and moral formation and discernment will always be part of the church's life and mission. This is to say yet again: in the church's own struggles for justice, peace and the integrity of creation, the *esse* of the church is at stake.[29]

72. A further implication is that the boundary between moral formation in the church and moral formation in the world is fluid. We noted in paragraph 16 above some important results of the churches' common struggle with ethical issues (for example, the affirmation of the fundamental equality of women and men, and the need to exercise a responsible stewardship of the environment). Yet these results have also come as the churches interacted with moral struggles in society, struggles in which the church has learned as much as it has taught. In this sense the efforts for moral formation in society have had an ecclesial significance: through these efforts the church has learned how better to *be* church.

73. Here the language of moral formation and discernment relates to our earlier discussion of "koinonia-generating" engagement in ethical issues. We see that moral struggle, discernment and formation are not optional "extras" alongside the understandings of church which come from our various traditions. They also *challenge* those traditional understandings, helping us learn from God's world how better to be church. As noted in paragraphs 35-42 above, the community born in the cooperation of people of goodwill working for a peaceful, just and sustainable world may not be ecclesial *per se*. But it has ecclesial consequences insofar as it is the agent of God's process of moral formation for the church itself.

74. We feel that the language of moral formation and discernment can be helpful in reflecting on many more areas of the faith, life and witness of the church: for example, the empowerment of the laity, catechesis directed to the formation of Christian conscience, a content and form for the church's social witness, and the linking of koinonia,

diakonia, martyria and leitourgia. At the same time, this language can help re-weave the "moral fibre" of society and contribute to its moral and spiritual health when both are in disarray. These matters need to be developed through a more thorough analysis of the process of moral formation and discernment. That task lies before us.

NOTES

[1] The report and papers from this meeting have been published in *Costly Unity*, Thomas F. Best and Wesley Granberg-Michaelson, eds, Geneva, WCC, Unit III and Faith and Order/Unit I, 1993. See also the report, on pp.2-23 of this volume.

[2] *Faith and Order: The Report of the Third World Conference at Lund, Sweden: August 15-28, 1952*, O.S. Tomkins, ed., Faith and Order Paper no. 15, London, SCM, 1953, pp.5-6.

[3] The statement, submitted to Section II on "What Unity Requires" of the fifth assembly of the WCC in Nairobi (1975), insisted that "an ecclesiastical unity which would stand in the way of struggles for liberation would be a repressive unity... We must resolutely refuse any too easy forms of unity..." See *Uniting in Hope: Commission on Faith and Order, Accra 1974*, Faith and Order Paper no. 72, pp.93-94.

[4] See note 1.

[5] *Church and World: The Unity of the Church and the Renewal of Human Community*, Faith and Order Paper no. 151, Geneva, WCC Publications, 1992.

[6] *On the Way to Fuller Koinonia: Official Report of the Fifth World Conference on Faith and Order*, Thomas F. Best and Günther Gassmann, eds, Faith and Order Paper no. 166, Geneva, WCC Publications, 1994.

[7] *Signs of the Spirit: Official Report, Seventh Assembly, World Council of Churches*, Michael Kinnamon, ed., Geneva and Grand Rapids, WCC Publications and Eerdmans, 1991.

[8] *On the Way to Fuller Koinonia*, *op. cit.*, pp.263-95.

[9] Para. 1, p.269.

[10] "The Unity of the Church as Koinonia: Gift and Calling", most recently available in *On the Way to Fuller Koinonia*, *op. cit.*, para. 3.2, p.270.

[11] Chapter IV, para. 32, p.49.

[12] Report of Group IV, para. 25. See *On the Way to Fuller Koinonia*, *op. cit.*, p.259.

[13] Para. 1.3. See *On the Way to Fuller Koinonia*, *op. cit.*, p.269.

[14] Report of Group IV, para 25. See *On the Way to Fuller Koinonia*, *op. cit.*

[15] Para. 29.

[16] *Church and World*, *op. cit.*, chapter III, para. 1, p.22.

[17] Santiago, Report of Group IV, para. 8. See *On the Way to Fuller Koinonia*, *op. cit.*, p.255.

[18] Faith and Order Paper no. 111, Geneva, WCC, 1982, "Eucharist", para. 20, p.14.

[19] Report of Group IV, para. 32. See *On the Way to Fuller Koinonia*, *op. cit.*, p.260.

[20] Para. 42.
[21] *Ibid.*, para. 44.
[22] Para. 19.
[23] "Eucharist", para. 20, p.14. See also paras 2-26, pp.10-15.
[24] "Eucharist", para. 1, p.10.
[25] "Costly Unity", see p.2 of this volume, para. 1.
[26] The final report from the study process may be enhanced by an excursus on biblical material relating to this theme.
[27] The final report from the study process may be enhanced by an excursus on biblical material relating to this theme.
[28] The final report may be enhanced by an excursus on the "Haustafeln" in the Pastoral Letters, including reference to John Howard Yoder's *The Politics of Jesus*.
[29] Cf. "Costly Unity", p.4 of this volume, para. 5.

List of Participants

Anna Marie Aagaard, Denmark
(co-moderator)
André Birmelé, France
Frans Bouwen, Israel
Emilio Castro, Uruguay
Emmanuel Clapsis, USA
Duncan B. Forrester, Scotland
(co-moderator)
John de Gruchy, South Africa
Vigen Guroian, USA
William Henn, OFM Cap., Rome
Bert Hoedemaker, Netherlands
Timothy Kiogora-Gideon, USA
Jan Lochman, Switzerland
Peter Lodberg, Denmark
Nestor Miguez, Argentina
Valamotu Palu, Tonga

Elisabeth Prodromou, USA
Larry Rasmussen, USA
Mary Seller, UK
Geraldine Smyth O.P., Ireland
Thomas F. Stransky, USA
Elisabeth S. Tapia, Philippines

WCC staff
Thomas Best, executive secretary, Faith and Order
Martin Robra, executive secretary, Economy, Ecology and Sustainable Society
Marise Pegat-Toquet, administrative assistant, Economy, Ecology and Sustainable Society

Costly Obedience

Johannesburg, South Africa, June 1996

INTRODUCTION

1. We come now to the final phase of our study of ecclesiology and ethics. We have explored the common ground and needed relationships between the historic ecumenical projects representing these two areas of interest. The tasks of Faith and Order and Life and Work now continue in the work of Units I and III of the World Council of Churches, which have together sponsored this inquiry.

2. At Rønde, Denmark, in 1993, we explored the relationships between koinonia on the one hand, and justice, peace and the integrity of creation on the other. We challenged the persistent division between the search for visible unity and pursuit of the church's call to prophetic witness and service. We asserted that the ecumenical movement "suffers damage" so long as it is unable to bring these discussions and processes into fruitful interaction. We spoke of the church as intrinsically a "moral community", saying that the church not only *has* an ethic but *is* an ethical reality in itself. We argued that ways forward from these insights seemed "both possible and promising".

3. At Tantur, Israel, in 1994, we surveyed continuing efforts to promote such relationships. We looked at memory and hope as foundations for the Christian life, explored the relation of movements and action groups to the structures of the church, considered the interactions of eucharist, covenant and ethical engagement, and took up the ecumenical dimension of moral witness. This time we avoided the term "moral community" and argued instead that in the church as koinonia a constant process of moral formation takes place. We looked for new terminology and found it in the biblical image of

oikos, the house or household of life, bringing together the ecological, economic and ecumenical dimensions of our lives. We said, "In the church's own struggles for justice, peace, and the integrity of creation, the *esse* of the church is at stake."

4. Now, in a meeting in Johannesburg, South Africa, 19-23 June 1996, we have further pursued the theme of moral formation, asking what it might mean to speak of the church as a global communion of moral witnessing. The obedience to which we are called is often costly. It may require the churches to position themselves in relation to the issues of particular times and places in ways which call for courage, perseverance and sacrifice. Such faithfulness may, as it has for some of our own contemporaries, come to the point of martyrdom. In memory the church celebrates its martyrs of both the distant and the recent past. In hope it looks for the fulfillment of the reign of God for which they stood. The great "cloud of witnesses" (Heb. 12:1-2), by which we are "surrounded" and whose obedience to God we are called to remember, summons us to a koinonia more profound than any that we have yet been able to achieve.

5. To Johannesburg we brought our diverse theological backgrounds and tendencies. But we were also influenced by having met at this particular place and time and by our shared experience of worship, study, debate and fruitful encounter with local church members and leaders. We were moved to have the opportunity of visiting South Africa in the time of its transition to democracy. We were warmed by the reception we received and impressed by the persons who turned out to greet us. We were saddened to learn of the growing unemployment and violence that have already overtaken this beloved country. We sensed that a political miracle now needs to be followed by an economic miracle. The latter will be more difficult to achieve.

6. We are struck by the perilous, yet hopeful, character of the human situation in which we live. It is easier to say that our moment in history is "post"-something — post-modern, post-apartheid, perhaps post-liberal — than to say what it *is*. We are rapidly becoming a global community, yet a community constituted by dehumanizing economic and political relationships. We live with violence perpetrated both in the name of justice and in the name of resistance to justice's demands.

7. The planetary scale of our human struggle presents challenges beyond any the churches have faced before.[1] Moral issues, formerly

seen as having to do mainly with personal conduct within stable orders of value, have now become radicalized. They now have to do with the life, or the death, of human beings and of the created order in which we live. Before we can even speak of a 21st-century "global civilization", life together on this planet will need shared visions and institutional expressions for which we have few really relevant precedents. As Christians we speak of an *oikoumene*, or inclusive horizon of human belonging, offered by God in Jesus Christ to the human race. Following the scriptures, we call this a "household of life", a "heavenly city" where justice, peace and care for creation's integrity prevail. But what may it mean to live lives in the here and now which manifest the first fruits of these gifts and act in anticipation of their fulfillment?

8. Christian faith, today as in the past, risks being captured for ethnic and nationalistic purposes. It risks being called on to help protect the privileges and ways of life of dominant classes. Our brief sojourn in South Africa has suggested to us that the former apartheid regime's theologically constructed defence of racial separation could become an unacknowledged precedent for violence by the rich nations of the northern hemisphere, facing as they do immigration pressures and economic demands from the south and the continuing threat of counter-violence from multitudes of the still-wretched of the earth.

9. If the church is to fulfill its calling to be a sign of God's reign in such a situation, it is imperative that it begin to understand itself as an ecumenical moral community. Hence the importance of the theme of moral formation. The church needs to ask how — with all its theological, liturgical and sacramental resources — it can *be* a community of relevant moral witness for such a world.

10. Our study of these issues is arranged in four parts: (1) an inquiry into the meaning of moral formation in church and world; (2) a reflection on the churches' moral failure in face of nationalistic, ethnic and economic violence together with a discussion of Christian moral testimony in the victory over apartheid; (3) an exploration of moral formation's grounding in the liturgy of the eucharist and in the implications of baptism; and (4) a discussion of the idea of an ecumenical moral communion and the possible role, in realizing that communion, of the community called the World Council of Churches.

I. THE MEANING OF MORAL FORMATION
IN CHURCH AND WORLD

A. Moral formation and "ethics"

11. The decision to connect ecclesiology with ethics by way of a study of moral formation has raised questions of terminology that need initial clarification. In many languages (and many ecumenical documents including this one) the words for "morality" and "ethics" are close synonyms. Certainly the choice of the word "ethics" in the original plan for this study was not meant to close off the attention we have now given to "moral formation". Still, there is an important distinction to be made. "Morality" refers to patterns of actual conduct, while "ethics" refers to systematic, often academic, reflection on that conduct. "Moral reflection" or "moral reasoning" can then refer to the thoughtful formulation of rules of conduct in the context of given traditions of life or spheres of communal experience. "Ethics", on the other hand, is a field of study which seeks conceptual models for reasoning about the perennial moral questions of human existence, as well as dilemmas emerging in our century for the first time.

12. Many scholars in the field of "ethics" now search — independently of particular religious or ethnic traditions — for principles which can help us deal with the hard questions that arise for human beings as such, whatever their communal loyalties or backgrounds. This is a necessary enterprise for human well-being. Most of us live in situations where a plurality of religious and other life-traditions makes it morally (as well as politically) impossible to build public policy on the moral reasoning offered by any one of them, or even on a supposed "overlapping consensus" representing many of them. Yet urgent issues arise which need for practical purposes to be resolved. The typical work of a hospital "ethics committee" is a case in point: e.g. Shall life support for this patient be terminated or not? Shall this patient receive a heart transplant ahead of that one? Ethicists deal with such questions by seeking to establish principles for "post-conventional", and therefore potentially universal, forms of moral discourse. Such secular styles of ethical reasoning tend to relegate religious traditions as such to the private sphere. Safely insulated from the public world, these traditions can then be recognized as useful in forming people who will turn out to be good citizens. But traditional understandings of life are not, or at least not explicitly, considered

appropriate points of reference for settling questions which these citizens will face in the public realm.

13. It is important for the Christian thinkers to be in touch with this contemporary search for a consistent "post-conventional" ethic. Significant issues of human well-being are at stake. Indeed some "Christian ethicists" today work mainly in this frame of reference, understanding it as a Christian duty to participate fully in humanity's search for the meaning of goodness, or principles for living together in peace on this planet with respect for the dignity of all persons. Yet it is clear that this quest for some sort of universal secular moral discourse — despite agreement on many practical matters such as the defence of human rights — has thus far failed to find common philosophical ground. Indeed, many of the questers have now largely abandoned the attempt to find foundations, in the sense of reality-grounded first principles, for moral argument. Increasingly it becomes clear, even to some practitioners of the genre, that many putatively "post-conventional" moral arguments are not tradition-independent at all. Rather, they covertly interpret values embedded in the cultures to which the thinkers in question belong. Even for ethicists who proclaim their allegiance to a purely secular rationality it seems that "moral formation" of one sort or another plays an indispensable story-telling, symbol-making and motivating role.

14. It is the more ironic, then, that increasing numbers of secular thinkers are heard to complain that "Christian ethicists" who concern themselves with public issues have little to add to what one hears from the general run of thinkers indebted to the long tradition of liberal thought in Western modernity. Some secular ethicists are now saying they long to hear a distinctive note, something fundamentally different, something that could *make* a difference, from Christian colleagues. We need *both* to participate with others in the effort to articulate the public good *and* to find ways of speaking and acting publicly out of the riches of a distinctively Christian moral formation.

15. Formation within a particular faith community can generate indispensable resources for interaction with the world: it can help the faithful discover certain more generalizable ideas and foundational principles of moral life. The different Christian traditions have conceived the link between specific moral formation and generalizable ethical principles in different ways. These go back to different understandings of the church, and indeed to different ways of relating ecclesiology to christology. Where the church is understood as a new

divine-human reality, as in the Catholic and Orthodox traditions, the bridge from formation to ethical issues is possible only by way of a sacramental understanding of the world. The Reformation's grounding of the church in the faith-creating word maintains the "infinite qualitative distinction" between God and human beings and hence also between God's justice and human justice. It is sceptical of attempts to base ethical reasoning in ecclesiology. The link can more easily be made on the basis of the ecclesiology of discipleship found in "free church" thinking, where ethical decisions are seen as having directly to do with building God's kingdom.[2] In each of these cases our task may be interpreted from the standpoint of Christian faith as the articulation of an interdependence graciously given with human life. We live in a constant struggle to show that the generative story of faith is at home with varying secular enterprises for giving meaning to the human condition.

16. Attention to Christian moral formation is thus important not merely for clarifying our minds about what we are doing in the world as persons of faith. It is also important for Christian participation in the wider dialogue of humanity. We must ask how a distinctively Christian moral formation — with its grounding in the family, in catechesis and in sacramental liturgy — can relate to today's dialogue designed to clarify and help reach out towards the good for the whole human community.

B. The meaning of "moral formation"

17. What is meant by "formation"? Moral formation is a nurturing process in which a certain sense of identity, a certain recognition of community, and a certain pattern of motivation, evolve. Such formation can be the gradual work of culture and upbringing, or it may be self-conscious and intentional. Any community of which we are members "forms" us in the sense of orienting us to the world in a certain way, encouraging certain kinds of behaviour and discouraging others. A focus on formation points us towards emphasis on actual communities with their cultures: towards what anthropologists call the complex "thickness" of lives actually lived.[3]

18. The "formation" discussion inevitably turns sooner or later to the subject of "spirituality". It does so because this term no longer refers only, as it once did, to specific meditations and practices explicitly focussed on the self's relation to God, most often lived out by members of orders and a few other very special people. With

modernity's characteristic "affirmation of everyday life", [4] "spiritual- ity" has also come to mean the depth dimension of daily existence cultivated by both meditative and moral practices. The meditative and the moral, indeed, cannot be separated. They are part of one whole cloth. Spirituality can now mean the whole shape, the shared fabric, of our lives in God.

19. There are many specific traditions of Christian spirituality, each with its characteristic practices and exercises, each with its characteristic understandings of the link to moral life. And Christian spirituality is not the only kind. There are spiritualities related to the great world religions, spiritualities representing indigenous religious communities, and spiritualities promoted by individual teachers who operate, as it were, at large. Christian spiritual-moral formation in today's world needs not only to draw upon the riches of the great traditions of Christian faith but also to meet, understand, grasp its differences from, and perhaps learn from, spiritual traditions outside of Christianity.

C. Moral formation in the church

20. Moral-spiritual formation in the church is of a distinctive kind. Effectively or not, with better or worse outcomes, Christian congregations engender certain ways of seeing life just by being the kinds of communities they are. Indeed it is evident that ecclesiasti- cal polities play out in certain forms of life, certain ways of living, which shape the way church members comport themselves in the world. There is no way of talking about "Christian ethics" without asking how the congregation functions in moral formation. We are asking about the actual thinking that goes on in these worshipping communities and about their capacity to shape peoples' patterns of action. We are "formed" in specific ways in the community of faith, by its liturgy, its teaching the texture of its common life.

21. Moral formation in the church seeks to generate communities in touch with the world and all its problems yet shaped in a daily telling and retelling of the Christian story. Such formation makes generation after generation of disciples. Discipleship finds resources in many complexly interacting elements of churchly life: the education of lay persons, the preparation of pastors, moral discourse in family and congregation, the experience of seeking to serve the wider community. Liturgical formation, in the Lord's supper and in our

common baptism, is fundamental to all other kinds of formation and is therefore developed in more detail later in this paper.

22. Such shaping and nurturing go on whether we focus our attention on formation as such or not. The ways the church is ordered, its internal habits, its interactions with the society around it, all have moral consequences. In this formational sense, then, no one can deny that ecclesiology and ethics go together. To be in the Christian community is to be shaped in a certain way of life.

23. Yet there are certain cautionary observations to be made. It will not do to be unduly romantic on this subject. In the first place, for most of us, to speak of "formation" in the congregation is more challenge than accomplishment. We are not doing it very well. Most Christian congregations today, especially in the West, are in fact not very effective communities of moral nurture. Under the fragmenting pressures of modern life, we are not transmitting tradition from one generation to the next. We are suffering a grievous loss of biblical literacy. The present generation may be far less "formed" by the churches in scripture and apostolic tradition than at any time in the recent past.

24. Secondly, by taking seriously the duty of pastors and congregations to bring people to serious moral awareness, we are tying ourselves to whatever proves to be possible in this regard. Attention to formation within communions and congregations sometimes reveals just those regions of entrenched habit which are most resistant to fresh theological or moral thinking. Is it possible to base a socially engaged Christian ethic, say in opposition to apartheid or in favour of justice, peace, and the integrity of creation, upon the formation that most congregations in our time are likely to receive? In the present state of the church in many places is not what we do "malformation", or simply "non-formation", rather than genuine training in the faith?

25. And finally, an emphasis on moral formation is likely to disclose potentially church-dividing differences among the communions, as well as divisive tensions within particular churches, that have not previously surfaced in ecumenical discussion.[5] On the one hand, to the extent that these disagreements underlie more public ecclesiological differences, the study of formation may illumine the ecumenical enterprise. But, on the other hand, we may discover that these entrenched, often unspoken, assumptions pose more severe challenges to the unity of the church than familiar kinds of ecclesiological or confessional diversity. We are still ill-prepared,

with our present methods of ecumenical discourse, to deal with such issues.

D. Moral formation in and by the world

26. Whether or not the congregation succeeds in creating a significant moral culture for its members, a more general kind of formation is at work in our lives all the time. The world forms us through the shaping influence of its principalities and powers. The growing and ramifying global economic nexus colonizes our human life-worlds, reducing human thought to cost-benefit calculations, further impoverishing the poor and the poor in spirit, spreading the virus of consumerism across the earth.

27. Much of the literature of congregational life sounds as if the congregation were a total cultural environment, as if it were possible to take up the world's story entirely into the Christian story or, alternatively, to exclude worldly concerns as totally as possible. But totally monocultural communities scarcely exist in the contemporary world. Most of us exist in a multiplicity of cultural environments, and engage in several different occupational and familial practices, each with its own symbolism, logic, customs and the like. Pluralism enters our personhood. We are literally multiple selves, formed in different, and perhaps divergent, ways by our lives in the church, in our families, in our secular occupations, and perhaps in political, recreational or other activities as well. Each of these spheres of life is a distinct culture in its own right. The relation of the community called church to all of these other cultural situations varies from place to place, but the problem is unavoidable. "Ecclesiology" as this term has customarily been understood includes only part of the setting for faithful life.

28. To recover anything like the "forming" role the church once had would have to mean restoration of the sorts of one-possibility religious communities that existed in pre-modern times. That is not likely to happen short of some disaster wiping out the structures of the modern world. What people need and want is guidance in living their daily lives, exposed as they are to the corrosive pressures of state and market, to the beguilements of many alternative life-styles. We need to find a way to integrate personal moral issues with questions of social ethics and the public weal.

29. We have not made clear at the level of congregational life what a moral strategy for life in the household of God would look like.

Many persons of faith simply do not recognize the sort of moral engagement we have in mind as a vocation for themselves. Conversely, many of the most effective Christians in the world's struggles have difficulty relating their moral and political convictions to the faith they are being taught in church. In ecumenical organizations, our preoccupation with global strategies and large ideas may well divert us from the "parish pump" responsibility of making sense of all this for the average Christian on the ground.

E. Churchly and worldly formations in interaction

30. The powers of worldly formation often impinge upon the church before the church has much chance to impinge upon them. This happens not least through knowledge of morally significant events in the public world, including the religious and cultural symbols connected with them, transmitted through the media. The church's relation to such public information can be positive, especially when pastors are well-informed and alert to make appropriate connections. We said at Tantur, indeed, that the world has at times taught us how to *be* the church. We may learn from movements in the world what it is that the Christian tradition truly stands for. Some of our most significant acts of witness have "been drawn out by moral struggles in society in which the church has had to learn at least as much as it has taught. In this way the efforts of moral formation in society have carried their own ecclesial significance...." And, further, "there is something crucial here: moral struggle, discernment and formation are not simply to be 'annexed' to our understandings and ways of being church and used to draw out the genuine treasures of our traditions. They also challenge those deeply and teach us to learn from the world (which is, after all, God's) how better to recognize and 'be' church as a faithful way of life."[6]

31. There are, of course, consequences of this sort of learning. Societies, nominally "Christian" and otherwise, have indeed sometimes enacted what the churches — beforehand, at the time, or later — saw to be part of the genius of their own message. The outlawing of slavery and child labour, or the establishment of universal public education, are examples. But the secular success of church-instigated or church-backed policies has often set social processes in motion which in time leave the churches marginalized. Schools, hospitals, human rights laws and the like have often gained independent momen-

tum on their own and have abandoned their original ecclesial and
moral roots.

32. Finding themselves shunted aside by such secularizing processes, churches have sought other ways to remain socially involved.
Sometimes they have begun to reflect in their own lives the institution-
ally secularized forms of their original theological insights. They have
relearned their own messages from the world: but in thinned-out and
distorted forms. Victims of their own success, they have become
captives to current cultural interpretations of faith rather than places of
genuine contemporary formation *in* the faith. They have taken over
distorted ways of "reading" reality, and then, as a second step, tried to
elaborate such distortions theologically. The result is not formation in
the faith but "malformation". In a generation or less the distinctive
outlines of the faith have begun to disappear. [7]

33. This is especially true in situations, such as North America,
where a vaguely christianized "civil religion", as well as vaguely
christianized forms of popular religion, are transmitted and in a certain
way authenticated in peoples' minds by the media. Media presenta-
tions of Christian faith indeed may be virtually "irreformable" in that
protests and corrections are of no avail against deeply ingrained
images and assumptions. Films and "soap operas" — now also
distributed across the globe — are often more powerful sources of
information, and misinformation, about the faith than our own educational efforts among the people of God.

34. Here, as in so many other cases, ecumenical ties are all-
important for maintaining identity in the faith. Our awareness of the
challenge we face in forming congregations faithfully inevitably leads
us towards a deeper understanding of what ecumenism can mean in
action. We need the kind of formation which will help local communities to remain ecumenically aware under the pressure of events
which contain both threat and promise. We need to learn from
success, and also from failure. Can a distinctive, shared ecumenical
formation come to exist under specific local circumstances? Can it
come to exist globally?

35. The church bears moral witness simply by being what it is in
its human environment. By being what it is, it bears witness to some
message. It may stand for justice, peace and the care of our planet,
or it may stand for something else. We need to make this inevitable
moral witnessing self-conscious, and bring it under the control of the
story of faith. We need, in short, to make our formational activity an

intentional mutual upbuilding, an *oikodomé*, of the household of God.

II. FORMATION AND MALFORMATION
IN OUR ENCOUNTERS WITH THE PUBLIC WORLD

36. The church does not practise formation in abstraction from its history. The experiences congregations encounter in trying to find their way are themselves formational. The memory of past experience, including the experience of moral failure in the face of challenges such as those of nationalism, ethnicity, racism and violence, needs to be taken into our consciousness. The power of the community of faith to bear moral witness in society rests not only on its inner life but also on the outward roles it has played, and may in the future be challenged to play. A church not positioned where the gospel demands it to be amid social forces and events will *mal*-form its members, rendering them insensitive to the demands of their faith. Churches need ecumenical relationships, with the global accumulation of experience those relationships make available, in order to find an adequate perspective.

37. These thoughts need concrete illustration. We need to observe some respects in which the churches have failed to locate themselves rightly in relation to historic issues, and some instances in which the churches have, by the grace of God, better fulfilled their callings. We draw the examples given in the next few paragraphs both from recent European history and from the recent history of South Africa.

A. Malformation: Moral failure in the face of ethnic violence and warfare between nation-states

38. There has been a recurring failure on the part of the Christian church to prevent the outbreak of violence and war between ethnic groups and nations which have a Christian heritage. This does not gainsay some measure of success, but examples to the contrary prove the more general rule. The most obvious is undoubtedly the saga of war between "Christian nations" in Europe, where churches have not only failed to prevent war but have provided its legitimation. This was true in our century in both world wars and, more recently, in the former Yugoslavia. Similar instances can be pointed to in other parts of the world, often connected with European colonialism, as, for

example, in the Anglo-Boer war in South Africa (1899-1902). The tragedy is that the causes of such violence are seldom dealt with, and so the past, instead of being transformed, returns with vengeance to haunt the present and threaten the future.

39. Prior to the outbreak of the second world war, perceptive European ecumenical leaders, notably at the second world conference on Life and Work at Oxford (1937), warned their churches and governments that nationalism was threatening to engulf the European continent in another conflagration. The deep-seated national hatreds and social contradictions in European society which had led to war in 1914 had not been resolved or healed at Versailles. Rather, they had intensified, leading to the rise of Nazism and fascism and rapid rearmament throughout Europe. Churches were urged to act in a timely manner and together within their particular nations to prevent another war. Their pleas proved futile. This raises serious questions about the extent to which the churches shape the morality of their constituencies and, in turn, exert an influence on their nations, especially those which claim to be Christian.

40. Despite the prophetic voices of some Christian leaders, churches often seem powerless or unwilling to counter those forces within their countries which lead to ethnic violence and war. This points to a long-term failure to shape and form their constituency in ways consonant with the gospel of Jesus Christ, especially when this conflicts with national or ethnic self-interest. Churches often do not recognize, or else they abnegate, responsibility for moral formation, except at the level of personal ethics. Instead of being agents of just social transformation, churches too often uncritically conform to unjust social and economic patterns within their cultural and national contexts. The result is moral malformation of the membership of the churches, which inevitably has a similar influence on the wider society. This was notably the case in South Africa where British colonialism and Afrikaner nationalism aligned with racism and settler self-interest so penetrated the life of the churches that the majority of white Christians came to accept apartheid as right and divinely ordained.

41. Of particular concern is an inability on the part of the churches to learn from the history of such moral failure and, concomitantly, an inability to seek ways in which this can be overcome in the present. There seems to be a lack of will to remember, take responsibility for, and deal with the past in ways which will lead to national and

international healing. As a result, the demonic forces which are periodically unleashed are seldom countered in time if at all, even once there is a subsidence of the violence or the achievement of some kind of peace. Under such circumstances the peace achieved is uneasy, and there is always an awareness that war, like a medieval plague, will recur in the future given the right catalyst. The bitter cycle of violence which threatened to destroy apartheid South Africa in a racial war prior to 1994 is sufficient testimony to the danger of trying to achieve reconciliation without seeking to address the moral issues at stake.

42. There are many forces currently operative around the world which carry the seeds of violence, just as there are many contexts in the world today which are virtually in a perpetual state of violent conflict between ethnic communities and nations, often with religious support. The nature and extent of these forces have frequently been identified in ecumenical documents to which the churches have often paid no more than formal acknowledgment. These forces, or demons, need to be recognized now and named by the churches within their local contexts. They urgently need to be countered through a commitment to the values of the reign of God. Certainly, the churches in South Africa have begun to recognize their moral failures in the past, and how long it took before they discerned the sin of apartheid and confessed that its theological legitimation was a heresy.

B. Formation towards truth and reconciliation: the anti-apartheid struggle and its aftermath

43. Although the racial captivity of the churches in apartheid South Africa is a potent reminder of moral malformation, it is equally so that the role of the church in the struggle against apartheid, and now in the struggle to establish a just democratic society, provides an example of how moral formation within the life of the churches can take place and contribute to the ending of ethnic violence and the enabling of social transformation. Without romanticizing the church struggle against apartheid (there were, after all, many Christians and some churches which supported apartheid, and many others who remained silent when they should have spoken and acted), and recognizing the role that the international ecumenical community played in the process, it is clear that the churches and ecumenical agencies played a significant role in the ending of apartheid and the creation of a new South Africa. In hindsight it is possible to discern

the extent to which the church struggle, and its attendant suffering for the cause of truth, contributed to the moral and ecumenical formation of many people with regard to the issues of justice and peace. The churches are now faced with the enormous task of helping to create a moral culture which will enable South Africa to overcome the legacy of apartheid fully, and provide the basis for a society of lasting peace. With deliberate intention, through their community and liturgical life (including preaching, teaching and praxis), the churches have to deal with the past and seek to equip people to act and behave in public life as disciples of Jesus Christ.

44. We would like to highlight here the importance of the present Commission on Truth and Reconciliation in the social transformation of South Africa, the significant role of the churches and other faith communities in its operation, and the extent to which the work of the commission may be regarded already as an instrument in the healing of the nation and the moral formation of its citizens. We cannot elaborate here on the work of the commission. What is of paramount importance for our purposes is to recognize that its major thrust is to deal with past ethnic and racial violence and conflict in South Africa so that reconciliation and healing may become a reality. Of course, it is recognized that the commission might not achieve all the goals which have been set for it, and there is no way in which guarantees can be built into any situation to ensure that the seeds of violence sown in the past will not take fresh root and spawn yet another outbreak of conflict.

45. The commission was established by the government at the beginning of 1996 (thus within eighteen months of its election to power) and has been given only two and a half years to complete its task. This sense of urgency, as well as commitment, is indicative of the will to deal with the past with deliberate speed. Moments of grace have to be grasped when they are offered. The longer dealing with the past takes, the fewer become the options for overcoming its conflictual legacies, and shaping a more just and peaceful future.

46. Although the commission has been established and funded by the state, it is free to act on its own without any interference from the state or political parties and organizations. Furthermore, it has been given substantial resources with which to accomplish its task. Of note is the fact that the seventeen commissioners, appointed after a long process of hearings, are representative of the broad political spectrum in South Africa, and that many of them are religious leaders, including

the chairperson, Archbishop Desmond Tutu. Moreover, it is already evident that the commission is committed to dealing with past human rights violations irrespective of party or person, an essential step in establishing its integrity and credibility.

47. At the heart of the commission's work is the enabling of victims of gross human rights violations during the past three decades to tell their stories and, in doing so, to discover resources which may enable them to forgive their oppressors. The telling of the stories is, in itself, therapeutic and morally formative and empowering, but it is also backed up by a programme of reparation where this is appropriate and possible. Also central to the work of the commission is the hearing of confessions of guilt on the part of perpetrators of crimes, and the granting of amnesty where this is within the mandate of the commission. In many respects, the hearings have a "liturgical" character in which the whole nation is intimately involved, and its future moral character is being formed. Day by day at the hearings, as well as on television and radio, memories of the past are being relived and healed through confession, forgiveness, and a commitment to restitution. The ritual experience is always painful and often shocking, but it is also full of grace, justice and hope. Some opponents of the commission argued that its work would open up past wounds and put at risk the process of national reconciliation. But the opposite is becoming apparent. The commission is providing a central focus for the liturgy of healing and the reconstruction of moral order.

48. After centuries of oppression and subjugation, of racial division and conflict, it is vital, then, that a new nation is built in which the past is transcended and moral values re-established. But that task will take time and much effort both now and well into the future. Various churches as well as the South African Council of Churches and other Christian agencies, as well as other religious faith communities, have acknowledged that they have a responsibility to assist in ensuring that the work of the commission achieves its goals. They have also recognized that they have an ongoing responsibility, even after the work of the commission has ended, to help the nation deal with its past, and to help in the building of a moral community of citizens. This is essential in the long term simply because the deep causes of past violence, not least those of racism and economic self-interest, cannot be resolved in the short term, and new factors inevitably arise in the course of history which can so easily undermine reconciliation.

49. Furthermore, the ecumenical church in South Africa is becoming aware of the danger that lurks in the new emerging national consciousness unless it is, in fact, informed by a critical national conscience. However important a sense of nationhood is for the building of the new South Africa, the churches recognize that they dare not become trapped in the new South African nationalism if they are to fulfill their pastoral and prophetic role within society. They are aware that they dare not forget the many lessons learned in the struggle against apartheid, or deny the ecumenical and moral purpose which was then generated in standing for truth, in keeping alive the hope of victory over evil and the establishment of a just society. Without the memory of the past struggle for justice, and the expectation of an even more just society, moral formation will lose its direction and motivation in the quest for reconciliation and peace.

50. The emphasis in these examples on recent events in South Africa of course reflects the setting of our meeting. But that does not detract from their ecumenical importance. On the contrary, the particularity of this material adds to its ecumenical impact. As we will see, the oikoumene is best understood not by trying to reach some generalized global vision but by fostering a worldwide communion of particular, local embodiments of acted-out, shared, obedience to the gospel. South Africa has given us hope that such faithfulness can take on meaningful, specific, local forms and lead to results that enrich human life. Yet we know that not every situation will give us such clear lessons or such encouragement. In each situation we need to find our own way, yet always in relationships of ecumenical support and accountability.

III. EUCHARIST AND BAPTISM AS CONTEXTS OF FORMATION

51. From whence comes the power to sustain the sort of moral witness required of Christians during the South African struggle against apartheid, and now in the process of nation-building? From whence comes the strength to stand against injustice and violence in any situation of local or global conflict?

A. Moral formation in the context of the eucharistic liturgy

52. The heart of Christian moral formation lies in worship, through which the story of salvation is re-enacted in the modes of

prayer, proclamation and sacrament. Worship together involves certain focal actions intrinsic to the shared life of faith, actions which centre, sustain and order that way of life. Ritual actions show the way. They are "rites which embody what is right". They are "the connective tissue in a shared way of life, the whole of which morally educates and forms". Many Christian traditions refer to the prayerful, biblically informed, and ritually cogent enactment of the story of God's way with the human race as "liturgy" or *leitourgia*. This Greek word itself originally had a moral sense. It meant the public charge to perform a particular public service, or *diakonia*. The connection is still present in the Christian understanding of liturgy. [8]

53. Liturgy, in turn, is the churchly continuation and fulfillment of the original formative process we call discipleship. On the road to Emmaus the bewildered disciples of Jesus encounter him, not knowing at first that he is the risen Lord. They hear the gospel story once again as Jesus interprets to them "in all the scriptures the things concerning himself" (Luke 24:27). This is the very story in which they themselves have been participating as disciples, already eating and drinking with Jesus and those among whom Jesus had ministered. Finally they recognize him, as he becomes known to them "in the breaking of the bread". In eucharistic worship, the experienced story of discipleship is taken up into the very life of the Trinity.

54. The liturgy looks back to the transfiguration which already anticipates the fulfillment of God's reign, and forward to the messianic banquet yet to come. It combines in its structure the combination of memory and hope which we have seen to be needed in actual situations of reconciliation. It ties memory and hope specifically to our participation in the story of Jesus. It effects a transfiguration of our lives. It enacts the presence of the Holy Spirit in the church, the human world, and all creation, now understood as participating in the historic economy of the trinitarian life. It invites human beings to participate with Jesus Christ, who has already carried our humanity into the Godhead, in the divine dance. This participation gives us new eyes to see the world and new energy to bear witness in it. Liturgy is thus not something added to moral and political endeavour but its nourishing ground.

55. The "Baptism, Eucharist and Ministry" study made this moral dimension of the eucharist fully explicit. "It is a representative act of thanksgiving and offering on behalf of the whole world." It is "a constant challenge in the search for appropriate relationships in social,

economic, and political life" (Matt. 5:23f.; 1 Cor. 10:16f.; 1 Cor. 11:20-22; Gal. 3:28). Furthermore, "All kinds of injustice, racism, separation and lack of freedom are radically challenged when we share the body and blood of Christ." And, "As participants in the eucharist... we prove inconsistent if we are not actively participating in [the] ongoing restoration of the world's situation and of the human condition.... [W]e are placed under continual judgment by the persistence of unjust relationships of all kinds in our society, the manifold divisions on behalf of human pride, material interest and power politics, and, above all, the obstinacy of unjustifiable confessional oppositions within the body of Christ."[9]

56. Indeed liturgy, understood in this broad moral as well as devotional sense, is the principal dialogic encounter where God and human beings meet: where the ecclesial body is knit together as a single cloth of narrative, teaching, repentance and forgiveness, confession and proclamation, prophecy and doxology. This cloth is woven on the extensive frame of an eschatological vision. Clearly, the character of the church as moral community is grounded in liturgy, but does not exhaust the liturgy's whole meaning. It is indispensable to locate moral formation here at the heart of the church's expression of its intrinsic nature, yet not to suppose that morality expresses the whole of that nature.

57. Yet it is important to see that liturgy, if not properly understood and acted out, can *mal-form* the church as readily as it can form it in faith. Liturgy and worship may well perpetuate or legitimate unjust arrangements both within and outside ecclesial boundaries. Serious attention must be given to the broader social context in which liturgy functions and to which the church belongs. Devotion to the liturgy has sometimes lent itself to an irresponsible ghetto mentality, has countenanced unjust social arrangements, or legitimated ethnic-religious violence. We have watched certain churches, liberated from the constraints of totalitarian regimes, enthusiastically embrace movements of recrudescent nationalism. Worship has sometimes been a rehearsal ground for violent expressions of nationalism against ethnic and religious minorities.

58. Thus it is for Christian moral awareness sometimes to purify the liturgy. But it is for liturgy in turn to give back to moral formation that eschatological fullness which only eucharistic worship can actualize. Several New Testament passages (e.g. Matt. 6:11-12; 2 Cor. 3:18; Rev. 21) point to the heart of the matter. Perhaps most

pertinent is Romans 12:1-2. Paul makes it clear that "a renewal of your minds" must happen so that Christian moral life is possible, so that we "might discern what is the will of God, what is good and acceptable and perfect". In this passage true worship *(ten logiken latreian)* is the pouring out of ourselves in service to others.

59. Liturgical worship keeps alive the capacity of Christ's story to break open and extend the possible ways of living as a Christian community. By connecting the fundamental Christian story with the very presence of the mystery it re-enacts, the liturgy has potential for overcoming the church's malformation and for transfiguring its view of the world and capacity for action in the world. Because this transformation is incarnational, not merely narrational, the world must deal not just with our stories but with our bodies. Repositioned in the world, we "read" the world differently, and therefore act there in new ways. We reinterpret and rearticulate symbols which function powerfully in relation to patterns of belonging and power.

60. It is important to see that this presentation of the relation between worship and witness in terms of "liturgy" has parallels in other Christian traditions, other Christian vocabularies. Our different traditions of eucharistic worship go together with characteristic forms of church-world interaction: ways of understanding Christian formation in the midst of the formative powers of the world. To be genuine manifestations of the church of Jesus Christ, these traditions need to participate in the ecumenical whole. Our forms of worship, however diverse they may appear, have much in common. In their essential forms, our liturgies tell the same story. Yet we need full appreciation of the particularities of diverse Christian traditions as coherent fields of devotion, discourse and action.

61. By asking churches to articulate their own particular ways of acting out the story of Jesus in the world, we invite them further into the ecumenical dialogue. Mutual enrichment, as well as mutual critique and correction, can occur when distinct traditions encounter one another. Soon we realize that single Christian traditions cannot exist in isolation. Traditions of formation inevitably overlap. All traditions of life grow and change. The possibility exists, as we have seen, that a given tradition of Christian formation becomes deformed or *mal-formed* by having internalized, given theological sanction to, and even worshipped local principalities and powers. Here ecumenical relationships can help churches recover the moral marks of apostolicity and catholicity they have lost.

B. Baptism as the sign of membership in one morally witnessing people of God

62. Nowhere is the ecumenical reality more evident than in the fact of our common baptism. In baptism we either enter upon or celebrate the same basic formation — in Jesus Christ's life, death and resurrection — despite differing eucharistic and theological expressions of it. The process of Christian initiation, whatever the order and timing of its constituent events (baptism, catechesis or instruction, personal confession of faith, confirmation), is our entry into membership in the body of Christ, and therefore into a transformative moral process. It is a crucifying of the "old Adam", by which the power of sin is broken. It is the sacrament of nurture of the life of faith in our hearts by the Holy Spirit. It is the inauguration of "growth into the measure of the stature of the fullness of Christ" (Eph. 4:13). It is "transformation by the power of the Holy Spirit into his likeness" (2 Cor. 3:18). It is liberation into a new humanity. It is a sign and seal of our common discipleship.

63. Moreover, in the act of baptism there are clear formational responsibilities indicated for the entire community of faith. Parents promise to bring up their child in the nurture and admonition of the Lord. The whole congregation pledges itself to provide an exemplary environment of witness and service. Within, and beyond, the community of faith those baptized are led into a life of moral witnessing. As the *Baptism, Eucharist and Ministry* document says, they are "pardoned, cleansed and sanctified by Christ, and are given as part of their baptismal experience a new ethical orientation under the guidance of the Holy Spirit". [10] And, further, "... baptism, as a baptism into Christ's death, has ethical implications which not only call for personal sanctification, but also motivate Christians to strive for the realization of the will of God in all realms of life" (Rom. 6:9ff.; Gal. 3:27-28; 1 Pet. 2:21-4:6). [11]

64. Baptism is a local event with ecumenical implications. It is at once the rite of entry into membership in the local congregation and into membership in the universal church. We have come to the point of very widespread acceptance of one another's baptisms. Does this not also imply a sense of common sharing in the formation which baptism implies? The theme of moral formation, so intimately tied to participation in the liturgy of the eucharist, is through our common baptism shown to be an ecumenically shared reality. Although there are many readings and interpretations of, a multiplicity of perspectives

upon, Christ's presence in history, our common acceptance of baptism shows us that the task of formation in Jesus Christ is inherently one, a task shared by the entire church. The discipleship into which we are initiated at baptism transcends denominational and confessional boundaries. We thereby enter into union with Christ, with each other, and with the church of every time and place.

65. How, in the midst of our divisions over ministry and the Lord's supper, can this baptismal-moral unity find a more visible form than it has yet achieved? We are not yet able to give it the visible form it inherently demands: unity in eucharistic worship. But may not the one baptism even now find visibility in the catholicity of a community of moral nurture and witnessing: an ecumenical community of costly discipleship? Baptism has to do with the *lived reality* of the new life in Christ, a community in which the gifts of faith, hope and love are received and practised. Therefore unity in baptism can have a visible *moral* form, even if it does not yet have a visible ecclesiastical form.

66. Furthermore, does not the mutual recognition of baptism imply a mutual recognition of members? And if so, does that not imply some mutual sharing of and responsibility for the formation of the people of God? In the formation of our own members are we not responsible for guiding them towards ways that recognize their responsibility for moral solidarity with Christians of other congregations, confessions and communions? Does not our common responsibility for baptismal formation point towards a responsibility for building up the people of God in every place? In view of our common recognition of the one baptism, the accompanying formation should include instruction in what this larger, "catholic" formation means. It should make our members aware that the formation they receive leads to a common responsibility, across all lines of ecclesiastical or ethnic difference, for being a people in the world that can make a difference. Baptism *is* the difference which makes a difference.

67. Ironically, the churches even now have not been able to find any significantly visible expression of this oneness among baptized, and therefore formed-in-Christ people. Yet to the extent that our formative efforts succeed, the resulting community of moral witness *is* an ecumenical reality needing nurture, concretion and recognition. A moral community of the baptized, struggling with issues of justice in the life of world, could, for now, be the most visible and tangible lived expression of the unity that is given us in Jesus Christ.

IV. TOWARDS COMMUNION IN MORAL WITNESSING

A. Transcending old vocabularies

68. We have been engaged in a study process which seeks to appropriate the achievement of two great ecumenical enterprises, yet also to break free of the dichotomy of consciousness and effort these streams have represented. This task needs deep understanding and appreciation of what Faith and Order and Life and Work have stood for over the years, and a desire that these enterprises should go forward in a shared perspective that sees their visions as richly inter-related. [12] Such a goal cannot be reached by simply pasting together in the same paragraphs sentences in each of these two institutional languages, seeking to say the same thing first in one vocabulary and then in the other. The point is to break away from the artificial division of perspective two distinctive vocabularies have represented. This calls for a vision, with language to go with it, that substantially recasts the two perspectives into one.

69. The time is right for such an attempt, not least because the WCC itself is about to undergo significant change. That change will not simply be a matter of bureaucratic reorganization (although there will be some of that) but hopefully the enactment of a vision representing a decisive forward step in the history of the ecumenical movement.

70. We must never make the mistake of confusing what an ecumenical enterprise stands for — its fundamental vision — with the particular institutional form and vocabulary used. No vision can work its power in the world, of course, without *some* vocabulary and institutional form. But given vocabularies always reflect specific institutional histories. They tie the "native speakers" of the enterprise to those histories. They carry codes which insiders recognize. The point is not to forget where we have been and how we got there but to find a new vocabulary which can take these visions up into a new synthesis: a vocabulary not burdened by the past yet capable of conveying the best of the past into a new era.

71. In the nature of the case, the new vocabulary we are seeking will not spring full-blown from any study report, least of all this one. It will be the product of shared ecumenical experience. If we learn to live together in a morally engaged worshipping community, we will eventually find the words to talk about it. Our reflections on the

church as intrinsically a community of moral formation and world-engagement are intended as a move in that direction.

B. A freedom to seek new patterns

72. Under what conditions are we seeking this new understanding? In some situations the church is still captive to long-standing cultural expectations which restrain fresh thinking and innovation. But increasingly, these cultural expectations are disappearing as secularized societies cease to have much notion of, or indeed to care much about, what the church may claim to be its role in the world. In some places there have never been any such expectations. More and more young people grow up without religious education. For them there is a *tabula rasa* so far as religious institutions are concerned. The upshot is that we are freer than we have been in centuries to be the church we believe God wants us to be, but the task of making that happen in post-traditional, secularized societies is likely to be monumental.

73. In some situations the pressure of circumstances gives the church few options. Overthrowing injustice or oppression, or sheer survival, may be the unavoidable agenda. But more often, and especially in the West, there are too many signposts, too many competing visions. It is hard for Western Christians to see their way, not because the territory is trackless but because there are too many possibilities, too many ways of seeing the world, which they are invited to consider as if they were spiritual consumers. The watchword is "choice", as if choice were the same thing as freedom.

74. Many in the West share the conviction that in this vertigo of possibilities the church has largely lost its way. Certainly many current ecclesial forms of life and thought fail to work very well. Some are manifestly dysfunctional. Yet there are signs of the future in our present patterns of practice, if only we can identify them for what they are. Can we break away from formulas of the past which prevent us from seeing the opportunities we have in this generation? One way to do so is to see that living the Christian story and bearing moral witness to it in the world are inextricably inter-related. Eucharistic worship, rightly understood, renders ecclesial and moral reality one.

C. Ecclesio-moral formation as the clue

75. We have sought the clue to what we must do now in the notion of formation in the faith, which today means a discipleship worked out

in a formation simultaneously liturgical and moral. We have seen what this means, both in terms of thought and in a concrete instance. It does not mean capture of the Christian message by any ideology: radical, liberal, conservative or otherwise. We need to find our way again not through choosing an attractive political vehicle but through recovery of the very substance of the faith as confessed and lived. This means, above all, a return to the sources, a deep revisiting and renewal of our connection to the story of salvation through its repetition in worship, where the enacted narrative manifests its transcendent dimension of mystery and becomes more than just another beguiling story.

76. Such formation compels us to a bodily form of witness, a moral positioning, an engagement intrinsic to the persons we have become in the community of faith. It likewise shapes the community of faith itself to take an intrinsically moral role in relation to events around it. All this is one reality, one process, one journey, one experience. Not first this and then that, but this single, integral, way of life, seeing, hearing, thinking, doing. Not first a theological moment and then a practical moment but one stream of life shaped by the baptismal call to discipleship and eucharistic memory and thanksgiving which open us to participation in the historical movement of the Trinity through the power of the Holy Spirit.

D. A focus on the immediate and the local

77. Of necessity, the life of faith understood this way focusses on the immediate necessities of our local situation, whatever that may be. Larger visions of history, even when they purport to translate biblical eschatology, may actually blind us to the needs of our neighbours next door, the concerns of our particular communities. At the very least, our reading of the signs of the times needs first to open our eyes to immediate opportunities for moral witness which can be grasped even when we cannot see very far or explore the larger ramifications of our actions. There are moments when the right action is apparent, when it is faithless not to act even though we know we cannot see all the consequences. Not all moral challenges involve risky "boundary situations". Too much reflection on general principles may even be a way of avoiding what we know full well is our immediate calling. Much of the time it is reasonably clear what we should do. We are to "do justice, to love mercy and to walk humbly" with our God (Micah 6:8).

78. In many such cases our actions are the result of formation which simply makes the move intuitive. We think in terms of values built into the sort of community we are. People so formed are not greatly helped by chains of abstract ethical reasoning. They confront challenges in terms of communal relationships, customs, kinship patterns, deep-seated convictions about what is fitting. They do their practical reasoning in terms analogous to the shapes of life lived in conversation with the scriptures and shaped by participation in the liturgy. Such formation gives us the preparation, the conditioning, the equipment, and the companionship to face the unknowable future which confronts us every day. In such circumstances, not to move to the side of a neighbour in need, across the street or across the world, would be a betrayal of the integrity intrinsic to our identity.

79. Yet not all moral challenges are so unambiguous as these. Acting out of a scripturally and liturgically formed integrity may not solve all moral dilemmas, or be without objective risk. There can be no guarantee that in the larger scheme of things we will turn out to be "right". Vaclav Havel makes a distinction between optimism and hope. Optimism is the mere expectation of success. Hope, on the other hand, does not mean we believe things will necessarily turn out the way we expect, or turn out well for ourselves in particular. Hope says there is ultimate meaning in faithful action however immediately ensuing events turn out. Indeed we see through a glass darkly. Many of the issues we face, as the Rønde meeting saw, involve life-issues of the most fundamental sort: issues of human life, issues of justice, issues of survival. It is legitimate to stand back and reflect on these things. When we do that our moral formation provides narrative, liturgical and conceptual materials for reflection. And we need also to be well informed about the situations we face and the thought of secular observers concerning them.

80. It is important to remember that thinking in terms of formation means that when we act it is the church acting in us, and therefore we have responsibility to act as witnesses in and for our community of faith. This means in the first instance that we act if possible with the support, the pastoral care of our own worshipping congregation. But further it means that we act in the context of the whole ecumenical church, in ways that are in touch with the experiences of others who have passed this way before.

81. In certain circumstances the action which appears to act out the integrity of our formed identity is one which takes us, and our

congregation, into a critical solidarity with some other movement in which we discern the Spirit at work, or the reign of God anticipated. Of course, it can be dangerous to think that we can objectively identify the Spirit's presence. But the criterion of the Spirit of Jesus Christ is that it proclaims that Christ has come in the flesh (1 John 4:1-4), and that means in accord with the story of the incarnation in which we have been formed.

82. One of the indications of the Spirit's working, as the Rønde consultation saw, can be the discovery of an intense koinonia in solidarity with others over issues of human importance. There is an enormous attraction in finding in the company of others more of that sense of koinonia of which our Christian formation has given us a taste. We want more, and sometimes find it in relationships beyond the visible church. But this is surely a principle to be applied cautiously. What we think is koinonia may be no more than a very human sense of companionship in facing danger and seeking adventure. Yet if the church is intrinsically a moral community acting in the power of the Holy Spirit, then it follows that living out its witness where the Spirit is also at work should extend the sense of koinonia that is intrinsic to the eucharistic community as such. We wrestled at Rønde[13] and Tantur[14] with this question of koinonia outside the community of faith. We still need more clarity than we have.

E. Reconstructing the oikoumene

83. Focussed as we are on many specific moral engagements, how do we recover a sense of the oikoumene? The description just given of moral struggle in each place sounds as if the local is all, and that the diversity of particular situations makes it impossible to generalize: as if no concepts of broad application can possibly grasp the many forms of "thick" particularity that mark the way traditioned, formed people exercise their moral integrity in each particular case. Does this localism mean that no general guidance can be given about what to look for? Is there no constant pattern in the way liturgically formed Christians should behave?

84. Not, it seems, in terms of moral propositions purporting to be universal in themselves. Rather, what we do is share the experience of the larger church, whose "locality" *is* the oikoumene, the inhabited earth. This is why the life of the ecclesia as moral community requires an ecumenical dimension. Every local moral challenge has a global

dimension. Every global issue has a local application. The complexity of such relationships is well set out in the Rønde document. [15]

85. But how are we adequately to articulate such things, and particularly such notions as the "global" or "universal", today? We face post-modernism's penchant for the deconstruction of all large systems of thought as well as the power structures legitimated by them. On the one hand, such deconstruction very properly attacks the pride of certain great syntheses of the Western academic world: syntheses that assume, for example, that objectivizing human sciences are forms of discourse superior to the "subjugated languages" of the poor and dispossessed. But on the other hand, such attitudes can be seen as demolishing, or at least undermining, the very notion of an ecumenical vision as itself a kind of global synthesis. Just at the moment we are trying to give ecumenism a new comprehensive meaning which might clarify the calling of the World Council of Churches; we find ourselves living in an age whose thinkers seek to dismantle all such large ideas. Our emphasis on formation, with its preferential option for the immediate and the local, seems in tune with the prevailing philosophical temper. But the very word *oikoumene* seems to violate this post-modern preference for particularity, evoking as it does the notion of the unity of the human race in the household of God. Can we still convincingly speak "ecumenical" language?

1. Resonance and recognition

86. We can in fact still recognize what certain words mean across great gulfs of cultural difference. The defence of "human rights" in many different contexts and cultures is an example. But, unless filled out in the "thickness" of specific local application, all such general ideas as justice, peace, the integrity of creation and democracy are likely to remain abstract, no matter how compelling their sound. And, such is the fragmentation of contemporary cultural existence that some of these words are beginning to lose the broadly applicable meanings we thought they had. Is this happening also to the notion of oikoumene?

87. One approach to answering this question could lie in recognizing the role of purportedly universal ideas or concepts as instruments of (often Western-based) power structures and turning instead to more inclusive and organic ways of thinking: ways capable of hearing and interpreting humanity's "subjugated languages". Such is the intent of what we now have to say about resonance and recognition.

88. The key insight is that the Holy Spirit generates a kind of energy-field characterized by the recognizable "resonance" of Christ's presence in the world. The identifiable presence of this resonance *connects* the many biblical and post-biblical forms of witness to Jesus Christ. God's incarnate presence in history indeed can be seen reflected in the ensemble of the many perspectives in which the spiritual, moral resonance implicit in Christ's life has been, and continues to be, known and appropriated by those who follow him. Each context of discipleship shapes us in a certain perspective on the world and thereby generates a community having a certain recognizable character. The Holy Spirit instigates an energy-field of resonance *among* these perspectives. [16]

89. Thus the notion of oikoumene is not to be understood as a globalizing, even imperial, concept appropriated from the ancient world as an instrument of subjugation by powerful churches of the West. It is rather to be seen as a conscious *mutual* recognition of the resonating patterns and configurations of activity that follow from the Spirit's working. Before there can be an articulable oikoumene there is the resonance in which diverse local communities of faith recognize and share the forming, energizing power of the Holy Spirit.

90. By choosing resonance and recognition as our metaphors we are able to turn to a biblical formula found in the Johannine literature. What goes on when we recognize the real presence of Jesus Christ in the form of a community? Is it like recognizing a familiar face? Like recognizing the pattern in a fabric? Perhaps the sense of "voice" suggests the kind of resonance we need. The sheep know the shepherd's voice (John 10:3; cf. Rev. 3:20). Voice includes the notions of timbre, tone, pattern, texture, characteristic turns of speech: the very factors that enable personal recognition. The voice of the shepherd is heard by the disciples and lived out in a personal communion with him. This communion is taken up into liturgy, where the rhythm of discipleship is included in the rhythms of the divine dance. Discipleship means hearing, being drawn, being formed, by the voice: not just its sound but also the content, the authentic note of a way of speaking by which we are shaped, attesting to an identifiable way of being in the world, yet a way of being having many different forms. It is this voice-pattern recognition that is celebrated, acted, co-risked.

91. The focus of ecumenical recognition is that the other community has an acted commitment analogous to one's own, and one's own

commitment is analogous to the other. The analogy exists because of a shared recognition-pattern of moral practice in the Spirit. People formed by the liturgical, that is worshipping, enactment of the story such that life in the world con-forms with that formation are able to *recognize* that others are doing the same: recognize that others "have the same spirit". Spirit is always something that realizes itself in concrete form, concrete life. We know it by how it looks and how it sounds. Such recognition is something holistic, never *merely* doctrinal or jurisdictional but also including both doctrinal and jurisdictional elements. It is recognition of the lived reality: a sense of moral communion. This is what oikoumene means.

2. *Markings*

92. Only when there is this resonance in the Spirit and the recognition in it of the voice of the shepherd do we have grounds for confidence that the words and symbols we use have sufficiently similar meanings that we are able to understand other communities of Christian faith, and that they are able to understand us, so that we can share liturgy and ultimately theological language with them. We are not talking about concepts thought to maintain constant meanings across all cultures. It may be that the only "universal" concepts are those maintained by the world's principalities and powers. We are speaking instead of words and other indicators embedded in, and deriving their meaning from, a formation in holy things lived out in moral witness. The terms "signs" or "symbols" come to mind. But these words have meanings in other contexts which could lead to misunderstandings here. Let us simply call our indicators of shareable sense in the midst of ecumenical formation "signposts" or "markings".

93. Certain signposts emerge in the process of living out identifying factors of moral formation. We may think of these as pointers that say someone has been this way before: what the Scots call "cairns" on the hillside. Someone has been here, and has called the goal of a process of costly and risky involvement on behalf of neighbours "justice". This contextual naming gives "justice" a thick network of meanings that cannot be conveyed until someone walks this way again. Or some community has called a painfully worked-out and costly concord among combattants "peace". Again, "peace" thereby takes on an experienced meaning for those who were part of this history. Terms like "justice" and "peace" function in the ecumenical movement to help persons with analogous experiences find one

another, and thus support, enable, encourage, and empower one another. [17]

94. The traditional "marks" of the church, grounded as they are in credal, liturgical and moral substance, function in exactly this way: as pointers which create a certain presumption that we, and all others who claim them, are grounded in the same resonating and recognizable community-forming work of the Holy Spirit. Our problem sometimes is that the articulable signs have taken over as substitutes for the lived realities to which they refer. Yet often we have little to go on but outward signs, expressed as they are in jurisdictional, confessional or doctrinal agreement, or in willingness to participate in conciliar relationships. Today we need to share more deeply the liturgical and moral substance to which the traditional marks and our practical interpretations of them refer. We have seen that one basis for such sharing lies in the reality of our common baptism. What may it take for our existing baptismal-moral sharing to become communion?

3. Communion

95. To be in communion means to be in a network of relationships such that the Spirit's resonance is shared and recognizable messages are given and received. Communion means a recognition that we are living the same stories in forms, both liturgical and moral, which manifest the mystery, the transcending ground, of what is historically manifest. That is why the story needs to be embodied not just in the telling but in liturgy. Liturgy lived out morally makes us participants in the Christian story in such a way that we are drawn into God's real presence. In liturgy we participate in making present the reality of God in Jesus Christ through the full trinitarian economy in history. This plays out in justice-seeking, peace-making, caring for our planet. Such acting-out generates the concrete reality of faith's active presence in the world.

96. To be in communion is precisely to be willing to share the liturgy in both its senses: as worship and as work. Communion is a readiness to celebrate the same liturgy, with the same moral implications, together, as we recognize one another in each place through resonance, recognition, and the presumption created by common markings. The ecumenical reality behind the institutional forms we give it is a network of mutual recognition of the pattern, or theme, or voice, of Jesus Christ among communities liturgically formed in him. It is concrete commitment to living out the story

which recognizes other, analogous, concrete commitments to living it out. Outside this network of mutual recognition, no particular local expression of church can be authentic. It is of the essence of the church universal to exist in this web of relationships, in which the local is all important but the ecumenical nexus of recognition is equally indispensable.

97. The communion we have with one another today is "real but imperfect".[18] The terms we commonly use to describe or test our communion are themselves imperfectly or incompletely understood. In fact they need to point to the fullness of ecclesio-moral reality we find in one another as we discern in one another signs of hearing the shepherd's voice. But as commonly interpreted, our theological language does not yet catch the moral fullness, the plenitude of witnessing presence in history, which completeness of communion requires. It is important not to drain the fullness from our language by defining our terms purely conceptually, juridically or ecclesiastically, and not also morally. Nor must we let some particular structural aspect of the church's life be considered the sole fulfillment of what this language means. All language related to communion points to the life, obedience, and liturgical-moral integrity of the community of faith in such a way that its world-relationships, solidarities and ways of being prophetic are part of that wholeness.

F. The World Council of Churches as marker and space-maker for an ecumenical moral communion

98. How do we make room on earth for this *oikoumene* of mutually recognized resonance among our ways of concrete moral-ecclesial being-in-the-world? The moral communion we have been talking about has as yet no obvious seat in space. No ecclesiastical jurisdiction exists as a place where the universal church in this moral sense comes to expression. All existing jurisdictions are partial both in what they include and in the depth of moral being they signify.

99. But some form of visible expression is needed if we are to nurture towards fulfillment the "real but imperfect" moral communion that already exists among Christian communities of faith. Some community which marks its possibility, which makes articulated space for its appearing in fullness, is needed. The World Council of Churches may well come closer than any other entity to being that mark and offering that space. It *is* not the moral communion of which we have spoken, but it *is* a community of churches praying to receive

the spiritual gifts which such communion in moral witnessing will require.

1. Rethinking the nature of the Council

100. Current discussion of the nature of the Council runs between seeing it as a purely programmatic instrument of the churches (thereby denying it ecclesial status) and seeing it as the reality of churches-in-relation (thus suggesting that it has an as yet undefined ecclesial character). But may not the choice between these alternatives be confusing and in the end false? Programmatic initiatives can interpret and express the ecclesio-moral realities of WCC member churches. And churches-in-relation may fail to realize the ecclesial intentionality inherent in their relationship. Can we move beyond the perennial dichotomy between the ecclesial and the programmatic, especially in the moral realm?

101. Perhaps we can in principle. It is not our task to become directly involved in the Council's current "common vision and understanding process". But it would be disingenuous to deny that our work is relevant to that effort. If we have anything to say on this subject we want to stay at the level of vision. Consequences for budget, structure and staffing are not our business. That said, we have some broad suggestions to make concerning the perspective in which all these matters might be considered.

102. The WCC needs to mark, maintain, indeed *be* a space where the ecclesio-moral communion of which we have been speaking can come to expression, where language is constantly sought to express the reality more fully, where common actions are conceived which embody the needed moral witness, and where an ecumenical formation takes place which gives growing density, increasing fullness, to it.

2. Moral communion and sacramental communion

103. But here a question arises which needs careful treatment. We have consistently connected moral formation in this report with the sacraments of baptism and eucharist. That, indeed, is our basis for calling the goal of this enterprise a moral *communion*. But many of our churches, despite cordial relationships, are not yet in sacramental communion with one another. Can there then be such a thing as an "ecclesio-moral" communion which avoids, or transcends, our dividedness in the sacramental origins of moral formation? Do such

deep divisions not call in question, at least for now, the very idea of a universal moral communion as much as they do the idea of a universal sacramental communion? Do we not have to wait for moral communion until our divisions at the level of ministry and sacraments have been overcome? And if at the sacramental level no moral communion is as yet possible it makes no sense to suggest that the WCC should, as a present programmatic initiative, "mark" or offer "space" for such a thing, much less claim some sort of sacramental moral character itself.

104. Our responses to questions like these will depend on our ecclesiological commitments. For some there is no doubt a deep dilemma. The more closely we tie moral formation to the sacraments the less easy it becomes to argue that something called "moral communion" can unite us while sacramental communion among us is not yet attained. Yet it is also possible to argue that the notion of moral communion, despite its connection with the sacraments, need not stand or fall with the degree of our unity in the eucharist. There is enough moral substance lodged in the reality of our common baptism to justify some sort of ecumenical space-making right now for that shared spiritual gift. And if this is so it follows that the World Council of Churches should help make actively visible this given, already existing, baptismal-moral communion among its member churches.

105. It can also be argued that moral communion is distinguishable from eucharistic communion in another important way. Moral communion has a worldly *telos*: it can only be fulfilled in some form of public witness which requires us to be in touch with broad human questions belonging to the realm of "ethics". Such questions today, as we have seen, are both radical in their import and global in their character. There is a commonality in the human questions that can only be addressed through an equally common Christian witness. Only an organization like the World Council of Churches can help its member bodies discern and act out the comprehensive human implications of their particular sacramental-moral-formational processes. The effort to do this can itself generate a koinonia of thoughtful, daring, costly witnessing. A kind of communion can come into being through this grace-enabled work itself.

106. There is a difference between seeing the Council as a eucharistic community in its own right, which few want to do, and seeing it as a place for this koinonia-generating response to the grace we have already received in baptism: this effort to think through what our different morally formative communions can mean to the world.

And if, in fact, the member churches of the Council can be brought to make such a commitment, the Council's very existence then "marks" or locates the reality of a growing moral communion: working out in concrete terms the meaning of mutual resonance in the Spirit marked by discipleship to Jesus Christ.

107. Some will wish to say even more. Some theologians will argue that an organization making space for such a communion in moral formation for worldly ethical engagement cannot stand entirely outside the reality it enables to exist. For those who take this view it follows that the Council participates somehow in the communion it helps to foster. The Council becomes an instance of that communion in a peculiarly comprehensive and communicative mode. It is a mark of the ecumenical community it gathers, and therefore in some sense is *of* the church, even if not churchly in the fullest sense.

3. Koinonia in the struggle for common witness: ecumenical affirmations

108. It is not possible to decide this last question in these pages, and for our purposes it is not necessary. [19] What is clear is that the question of the status of the Council as marker of a growing moral communion has a practical side. Can we do what needs to be done? The whole matter of communion in moral witness is moot if we cannot find enough agreement about the content of that witness to make the question relevant. Here a deeply ecclesiological question becomes in one respect a programmatic question as well. What happens when we try to give our hope for moral communion a moral substance? What can be learned from the history of attempts to do so? We will learn most for our purposes by looking briefly at the history of the "ten affirmations" produced by the 1990 Seoul conference and now carried over as a point of entry in the "Theology of Life" project.

109. The Seoul conference was intended by its organizers to help build a stronger conciliar fellowship in the ecumenical community around shared moral principles. Indeed, for some, the intention was to give such principles status as marks of the mutual commitment implied in WCC membership. The meeting was presented at the outset with an analytical document dealing with the challenges facing the people of our planet: a document thought by many to propose overly ambitious global reality-definitions couched in Western academic language too abstract to make contact with local experience in all its

variety and profusion. The conference instead produced a set of affirmations reflecting the contextual and ecumenical experience of the people present. Yet even this effort did not wholly succeed. In the aftermath a feeling arose that the "ten affirmations", grounded in actual experience as they were, still could not be given clear (i.e. unequivocal) meanings across a variety of contexts: that in different cultural and confessional situations their implications could not be foreseen.

110. One of the reasons for this reluctance to take affirmations home from ecumenical meetings is that, once we do, every proposition, even every preposition, connects or disconnects with local issues, both churchly and secular, and therefore with the power interests tied up in those issues. However subtle our reports from the ecumenical front, the defence back home of affirmations grandly adopted at world conferences can make us seem to be taking sides on matters never envisioned when the affirmations were drafted, battling on one side or the other of dominant local dichotomies, opting for this or that alternative with all its ecclesiastical or worldly political consequences. This may well be the last thing we want to do and in fact may distort the intention of the original affirmations. Here may be a hazard impossible to avoid completely. It may be part of the cost of obedient witnessing. But the experience needs to be understood. It is an aspect of the koinonia-generating struggle which the search for moral communion can involve.

111. Do lists of moral affirmations still have a positive role to play? At their best, they have a sort of heuristic power. They help us find the shared concreteness of our actual moral commitments in facing the most characteristic problems of our time. Lists of principles can help us discover the essence of the moral commitment that is present among serious formational communities at any given moment. They can help instigate the forming of more such communities and help deepen the communion among them. They can be carefully designed to resource local readings of what they mean. Skillfully interpreted by leadership, such affirmations can help churches at a distance from serious moral encounters concretize their solidarity with fellow Christians around specific acts of witness, for example the German womens' boycott of South African products during the period of apartheid.

112. But experience in this area has taught us to proceed with caution. Any such list of moral generalizations or affirmations must be

guarded against being merely a list, merely a talisman to be repeated by those who pride themselves on being alert to the world's ills and possibilities. Furthermore, moral catechisms can get out of date even faster than theological ones. There is always the danger of over-generalizing certain historical moments and analytical paradigms. This has happened, for example, in the widespread use made of the experience of the German Confessing Church and the Barmen Declaration. The differences between one situation and another may be overlooked. Indeed historical paradigms, as well as moral principles, can be used covertly to defend and protect certain power centres or programmatic interests in the church rather than to illumine our moral paths. Even to make normative the transition to democracy in South Africa could be dangerous if used as a paradigm where it does not fit.

113. Finally, the impulse to issue lists of moral principles designed to address the signs of the times raises a question about our implied eschatology. What, over all, do we think is happening in the world? Where, if anywhere, are there signs that the reign of God has come nearer? Do we find such signs in the seeming extension of human rights, or in the apparent advance of democracy, or in successes claimed by peacemakers, or in the dire warnings of environ-mentalists? Indeed, it is not easy to discern, from this ambiguous moment in history, whether the household of life is anywhere taking form, or the holy city of God described in Revelation 21 is in any way drawing nearer. Yet these images of the household and the city can stand as eschatological metaphors or regulative ideas to guide us as we try to find our way.

114. The "ten affirmations" live up to their affirmative name. They are profoundly hopeful because they presuppose that by God's grace something can be done about the state of creation and of the human condition. They are valuable indications of the content that ought to be found in a moral communion of ethical engagement with the world. But, above all, they themselves help create the kind of space needed for an effort to think out and live out what such a communion could require, an effort koinonia-generating in its own right. As entry points for the wide range of local case studies in the "Theology of Life" programme, they "serve as a preliminary defini-tion of the framework and space in which people can build up confidence and trust".[20] If "space" has any meaning in this argument it is a territory in which we trust one another and have confidence that

by God's grace something will come of our efforts. In this powerful sense, the "ten affirmations" and other affirmations like them help create moral space for the "mutual upbuilding" or *oikodomé* towards a common witness that now becomes a primary calling for the Christian churches of the world. [21]

4. The community of oikodomé: A communicative "third force" in the world

115. The World Council of Churches, if possible in concert with other ecumenical bodies, should continue to promote the mutual upbuilding of such a visible moral communion, towards a vision of the church as moral "household of life". For this purpose we need an enhanced communications system among churches, congregations, and persons committed to this vision. We are challenged by the world economic system's ability to send and receive virtually instantaneous messages concerning financial transactions across the globe. We face the obsolete yet still powerful system of nation states. A nexus of another kind needs to have its place in the world. A network of moral communication among the churches could begin to function as a kind of "third force" to counter the hegemony of purely economic and political energies. The initiative to create such a "third force" could include critical, provisional, alliances with others who seek compatible goals. The emergence of the very idea of such a liturgically formed ecclesio-moral community could give the ecumenical movement a new energy and substance.

116. At stake here is not merely the future of a particular ecumenical organization. At stake is the future of the church itself. For the vision we have sketched to have substance and staying power we need to give urgent attention to the renewal in our churches of the work of moral formation in obedient discipleship, and of the kinds of costly ethical witnessing in the world that depend upon it. Such renewal needs to be sought in every congregation, in every confessional family or communion, in every place, in every morally perplexing situation across this deeply threatened but beloved planet, our home and the home of all the living things we know.

NOTES

1 See Bert Hoedemaker, "Introductory Reflections on JPIC and *Koinonia*", and Lukas Vischer, "*Koinonia* in a Time of Threats to Life", in *Costly Unity*, Thomas F. Best and Wesley Granberg-Michalson, eds, Geneva, WCC, 1993, pp.1ff. and 70ff. See also Konrad Raiser, "Ecumenical Discussion of Ethics and Ecclesiology", *The Ecumenical Review*, vol. 48, no. 1, Jan. 1996, pp.3ff.

2 This analysis is adapted from Konrad Raiser, *op. cit.*, p.7.

3 The term "thickness", popularized by the anthropologist Clifford Geertz, is now widely used by human scientists to mean the full and multi-layered complexity of cultures. It admirably links up with the concept of "formation". We are "formed" in rich and enveloping environments, not merely by the "thin" concepts scholars derive from those environments.

4 See, for example, Charles Taylor, *Sources of the Self*, Cambridge, Harvard UP, 1989, pp.211ff.

5 The question of the moral attitude the church should take towards homosexuality — especially where ordination is concerned — has already been divisive. The action of Orthodox leadership in suspending their churches' membership in the American National Council of the Churches of Christ a few years ago over the issue of the Council's *entertaining* (the matter never reached the point of accepting) a membership application from the Council of Metropolitan Community Churches shows how quickly a moral question can take on ecclesiological significance.

6 *Minutes of the Faith and Order Standing Commission, Aleppo, Syria, 5-12 January 1995*, Faith and Order Paper no. 170, WCC, Faith and Order Commission, 1995, pp.97-98. The corresponding paragraphs in the *Costly Commitment* report are 72 and 73.

7 Thus many American congregations seem today to suppose that a message of personal freedom and self-development lived out in an individualistic consumerist culture is a tolerable translation of the gospel. This assemption is, in fact, a form of captivity. It limits, if it does not negate, the potential witness of a Christian moral formation.

8 This material is adapted in part from Larry Rasmussen, "Moral Community and Moral Formation", in *Costly Commitment*, Thomas F. Best and Martin Robra, eds, Geneva, WCC, 1995, p.56.

9 *Baptism, Eucharist and Ministry*, Faith and Order Paper no. 111, Geneva, WCC, 1982, "Eucharist", para. 20, p.14.

10 *Ibid.*, "Baptism", para. 4, p.2.

11 *Ibid.*, para. 10, p.4.

12 It is not to be overlooked that both Faith and Order and Life and Work have consciously sought to overcome this dichotomy in a variety of theological formulas: the church as sign, sacrament and instrument, intercontextual method, the church as mystery and prophetic sign, the notion of the *status confessionis*, and so forth. See, for example, Thomas F. Best, "From Seoul to Santiago: The Unity of the Church and JPIC", in *Between the Flood and the Rainbow*, comp. D. Preman Niles, Geneva, WCC Publications, 1992, pp.128ff.; Peter Lodberg, "The History of Ecumenical Work on Ecclesiology and Ethics", in *Costly Commitment, op. cit.*, pp.1ff.

13 See "Costly Unity", pp.15-16 of this volume, paras 42-46.

14 See "Costly Commitment", pp.33-36 of this volume, section III, paras 35-42.

[15] See "Costly Unity", pp.13-14 of this volume, paras 35-37, esp. the following from para. 36: "The 'local' means different things in different circumstances. It may mean a neighbourhood, or a nation, or a region of the world. And sometimes an issue may be global in its importance, yet not susceptible of any single explanation or formula so varied are its ramifications in different places. Sometimes a global issue is such that it comes to expression most clearly in some particular locality, whose Christian people then have special responsibility for defining its significance for the rest of the *oikoumene*. Sometimes an essentially local issue can only be clearly seen when its global aspects are grasped."

[16] These ideas are adapted in part from the thought of Michael Welker, whose name surfaced several times in discussion. See his article "The Holy Spirit", *Theology Today*, 46, April 1969, pp.4-20. Welker writes that the Spirit "restores solidarity, loyalty, and capacity for common action among the people". Likewise it generates a realm of "poly-concreteness" in which there can be a "multifaceted, reciprocally strengthened and strengthening process of cooperation..." We find this an excellent description of relationships within the *oikoumene*.

[17] Terms such as "justice" and "peace" of course also have rich contexts of meaning in secular moral and political philosophy, as well as in the common parlance of journalists, politicians and diplomats. While it is indispensable, as we have said, for Christians to be in touch with these secular worlds, there is danger that their terminology represents a covert hegemony of Western thought-categories in one way or another related to Western political and economic interests. The idea of deriving the meanings of "justice" and "peace" (and of course the "integrity of creation" as well) from an ecumenical sharing of contextual moral engagements is intended to help us escape the hegemony of interests disguised as moral principles.

[18] These oft-spoken words echo inexactly the language of *Unitatis Redintegratio*, the "Decree on Ecumenism" of Vatican II: "For [those] who believe in Christ and have been properly baptized are brought into a certain, though imperfect, communion with the Catholic Church." See Walter M. Abbott, SJ, *Documents of Vatican II*, New York, Guild Press, 1966, p.345.

[19] Deep and divisive ecclesiological issues are involved, and behind them lie philosophical questions concerning the relationship of act and being. It could turn out that such questions are not resolvable in the terms in which they are currently posed, and that only in sharing a new moral life and language, responding to the working of the Holy Spirit in our time, can we move beyond our current impasse.

[20] Martin Robra, "Theology of Life: Justice, Peace, Creation", *The Ecumenical Review*, vol. 48, no. 1, Jan. 1996, p.35.

[21] See, on the image of *oikodomé* or "mutual upbuilding", the treatment by Geiko Müller-Fahrenholz in *God's Spirit: Transforming a World in Crisis*, New York, Continuum, and Geneva, WCC, 1995, pp.108ff.

List of Participants

Anna Marie Aagaard, Denmark
(co-moderator)
Duncan Forrester, Scotland
(co-moderator)
John de Gruchy, South Africa
Mongezi Guma, South Africa
Vigen Guroian, USA
William Henn, OFM, Rome
Margaret Jenkins, CSB, Australia
Margot Kässmann, Germany
Frans Noko Kekane, South Africa
Lewis Mudge, USA
Elizabeth Tapia, Philippines

WCC staff

Thomas F. Best, executive secretary,
Faith and Order
Alan Falconer, director, Faith and
Order
Marise Pegat-Toquet, administrative
assistant, Economy, Ecology and
Sustainable Society
Martin Robra, executive secretary,
Economy, Ecology and Sustain-
able Society

Part II

Reflections
on the Study

Living in Truth and Unity

The Church as a Hermeneutic of Law and Gospel

DUNCAN B. FORRESTER

The ecclesiology and ethics study project arose as part of a sustained effort to overcome a deep tension in the modern ecumenical movement, and indeed in the lives of the churches. On the one hand there was a tradition that the way to unity was through doctrinal agreement — the traditional Faith and Order approach. It was held that doctrinal agreement, particularly in ecclesiology, would remove the real obstacles to Christian unity; ethical issues were secondary and here more diversity was allowable than in matters of doctrine. Thus some theologians believed that with the approval of the immensely significant convergence document "Baptism, Eucharist and Ministry" (1982) the last real obstacle to reunion had been removed. They were quickly disillusioned, as it gradually became obvious that unity required conviviality and a sense of needing one another and belonging together rather than simply formal confessional agreements, and that disunity was often the result of non-theological factors.

On the other hand, there were those who proclaimed that doctrine divides and moral struggle in the world unites; so that the churches should work together and would then find more commonalities in action than in doctrine or worship. This was often regarded as the Life and Work, or Church and Society approach.

But reality was, of course, more complex. On the one hand Christians were reminded, particularly by the German church struggle and the theological declaration of Barmen (1934), and more recently by the struggle against apartheid, that (as Visser 't Hooft suggested) there was such a thing as a moral equivalent of heresy,[1] that certain types of practice were radically incompatible with Christian confession, that certain ethical issues were church dividing. There was also a discovery that in ethical struggle alongside others there was often a real and profound new experience[2] of what it is to be church. The being and message of the church are at stake when it wrestles with great ethical issues.

This led the Rønde consultation which produced "Costly Unity" to distinguish "cheap unity", which "avoids morally contested issues because they would disturb the unity of the church", from "costly unity" which is the discovery — or recovery — of the churches' unity in struggles for peace and for justice, where witness and social praxis are in solidarity. The next consultation, at the Tantur Ecumenical Institute near Jerusalem, reaffirmed that there can be no ecclesiology without ethics and no [Christian] ethics without ecclesiology,[3] and the fifth world conference on Faith and Order at Santiago de Compostela declared:

> The being and mission of the church, therefore, are at stake in witness through proclamation and concrete actions for justice, peace and integrity of creation. This is a defining mark of koinonia and central to our understanding of ecclesiology. The urgency of these issues makes it manifest that our theological reflection on the proper unity of Christ's church is inevitably related to ethics.[4]

In this paper I intend to explore the relation of ecclesiology and ethics as a hermeneutical issue, attempting to show how ecclesiology and ethics mutually illumine, question and interpret one another. I will seek to "earth" the discussion in an outline of how the hermeneutical process works in the various levels or modes of being church today. And I will suggest that a good way of understanding the koinonia which the church seeks to manifest for the sake of the world is the idea of dwelling in truth and unity where faith and action are two sides of the one coin, and the truth is known and loved in the solidarity of costly unity, discipleship and obedience.

The church's life: a hermeneutic of the gospel

Bishop Lesslie Newbigin has spoken of the church as a hermeneutic of the gospel. "The missionary action of the church", he writes more specifically, "is the exegesis of the gospel."[5] The Ceylon minister and theologian, D.T. Niles, illustrates the hermeneutic process dramatically and in simple terms:

> It is a common experience in India or Ceylon, when an evangelistic team visits a village, that in the meeting that is organized the small Christian community in the village will be sitting in the middle while the Hindus

and Muslims will be standing all around. And, in that situation, the evangelist is aware that whereas he is pointing to Christ, his listeners are looking at that small group sitting in front of them. The message will carry no conviction unless it is being proved in the lives of those who bear the Name that is being declared. This village situation is the world situation too, and for good or ill it is still the Christians of Western lands who are sitting in the middle. [6]

Newbigin develops the image further, emphasizing that in a village in South India

> the local community *is* the local community. Your neighbour who lives in the next-door house is also the man you meet at work, in your leisure, on holidays and on work days. And even though Christians may be a small minority, the church stands in the village as a visible invitation to the whole community. [7]

In such villages the Christians rarely have a church building; they worship in the open or under the shade of a tree, visible to all. Here

> [o]ne administers the sacraments and preaches the word to a group of believers surrounded by a wider circle of those who do not yet believe, but for whom also Christ came. One speaks to all, and the words spoken to the church are heard by those outside. [8]

The message of the gospel cannot be separated from the actual, day-to-day life of the community of faith. The life and nature of that community is a hermeneutic of the gospel.

If it is true that others understand the faith in the light of what they know and have experienced of the Christian community, the church, so also Christians may not separate their understanding of the gospel and the law from the fellowship that is called church. All Christian theology is church theology. For the church is called to embody and manifest the law and the gospel, and in fulfilling this one task with two dimensions it manifests the fullness of life and the salvation that is promised in Christ. This is its mission, its calling, not for its own sake but for the life of the world and the welfare of the broader community. Stanley Hauerwas provides as it were a theological explication of Newbigin and Niles's model:

> The task of the church [is] to pioneer those institutions and practices that the wider society has not learned as forms of justice. (At times it is also possible that the church can learn from society more just ways of forming life.) The church, therefore, must act as a *paradigmatic community* in the hope of providing some indication of what the world can be but is not...

The church does not have, but rather is a social ethic. That is, she is a social ethic inasmuch as she functions as a *criteriological institution* — that is, an institution that has learned to embody the form of truth that is charity as revealed in the person and work of Christ. [9]

It is not surprising if a theologian feels somewhat uncomfortable with the position outlined above with the help of Newbigin, Niles and Hauerwas. It appears at first glance to suggest that the goodness, the virtue, the morality of Christians and the Christian church vindicate the truth of the gospel. Yet we all know that this does not happen, that the truth of the gospel is demonstrated *despite* the failures of Christians and of the church, perhaps specially *in* their failures and sinfulness. "Religion", said the British playwright Dennis Potter shortly before his death, "to me has always been the wound, not the bandage." [10] What if living with the wound, the failure, the brokenness of things shows the truth of the gospel rather than the moral triumphalism of the ethically "successful"? What if in the struggle, the suffering, the risky obedience we encounter truth and have a new experience of costly unity?

On the other hand it is, of course, true that morality is important, and that Christians are called individually and together in the fellowship of the church to reflect something of the life of Christ. In practice, blatantly and persistently immoral lives among Christians are understood as invalidating the gospel. Although Christians know that they are called to confirm in their "walk" the truth of the gospel, the actual lives of Christians, *our* daily behaviour, are an acted denial of the truth by which we claim to live. All Christian traditions, with their varying emphases, attempt to take the law seriously, and have systems of discipline for their members. But we are all grateful to know that despite us and our failures, the truth of the gospel shines forth; conversely and paradoxically, the most polished moral achievement does not provide validation of the gospel, but indeed the very opposite.

The gospel: ethics beyond "goodness"

Something other than goodness, or perhaps more than goodness is required of believers and of the church. Despite the popular misconception, the church is not an organization for the moral achievers, but rather for those who know themselves to be moral failures, sinners. Christian lives should mediate grace and holiness rather than goodness, or at least goodness as it is conventionally understood. Because

Christians are forgiven sinners who none the less remain sinners at the empirical level, and the church is a fellowship of forgiven sinners which is itself as a visible social entity sinful and defective, the lives of believers and of the church should point not to a goal of moral achievement but to the source of their justification, so that Christian lives are more celebrations of a justification which they have not earned than exemplars of virtuous achievement.

Christian ethics as church ethics thus points to grace and to a holiness which in fact transforms the understanding of goodness; it points beyond the once again popular "virtue ethics" to the source of goodness and of holiness which is outside ourselves and to which we can never attain by our own efforts. Holiness is a gift; and it is also a calling. The stabbing finger of John the Baptist in Gruenewald's great altarpiece in Colmar points to the One in whom holiness and goodness are to be found, the One who both gives holiness and goodness and calls us to be a good and holy people.

Hannah Arendt made what was to her a surprising acknowledgment, that "the discoverer of the role of forgiveness in the realm of human affairs was Jesus of Nazareth". [11] This insight she, mistakenly, believed to be only loosely related to the message of Jesus. It rather "sprang from experiences in the small and closely knit community of his followers, bent on challenging the public authorities in Israel". She thus correctly links the message of forgiveness and reconciliation with the community of the church, but sees this linkage as an impediment to, rather than a necessary condition for, the entry of forgiveness into the public realm, where it cannot but challenge and undercut both conventional notions of morality and ecclesiologies which regard the church as other than a fellowship of forgiven and therefore forgiving sinners, a fellowship which must in its teaching and in its life point to a truer, because divine, understanding of goodness, morality and justice. It is my contention that the whole Christian reordering of the understanding of morality and of goodness cannot be sustained as a kind of free-floating wisdom, but only as inseparably linked to the person of Jesus the Just One and to the household of faith.

The church cannot speak of the forgiveness of sins unless it receives it and practises it in its own life. Some years ago in my own church there was a bitter controversy about whether two men might be ordained to the ministry of word and sacrament. Both had been in prison for serious offences — in one case murder, in the other large-scale embezzlement. The case finally came for decision to our general assembly. The opponents of the two men's ordination argued that ministers must be people of unimpeachable morality and high ethical standing. It would be impossible, it was argued, for people with such a record of crime to act as pastors, or to have the social status of ministers of the national church. The candidates' supporters argued that ministers, like all Christians, should know themselves to be sinners, should repent, and should have some experience of God's grace. After a long debate, the assembly decided by a small majority that it really believed the gospel it proclaimed, and allowed the two men to proceed to ordination.

A friend of mine who was a prison chaplain told me that just after the assembly decision he was going around the prison. A prisoner came up to him in tears. He had been an elder of the church, he said, and his wife had just visited him. "Yesterday," she told her husband, "I went to church for the first time since your conviction. For now I know that the church really believes in the forgiveness of sins, and that you and I are accepted in the church fellowship." That is an example of how the church in its life can, at least tentatively, upset conventional legalistic morality and point to the source of grace.

Lives that show *holiness* are the best confirmation of the gospel that is preached; they redefine goodness, or at least question the adequacy of commonplace understandings of the law and of legal goodness. In Christianity the understanding of goodness and of virtue is transfigured along the lines suggested by the parable of the Pharisee and the publican, and many another place in the New Testament.

The gospel: ethics beyond individualism

It is of the greatest importance that Christians are not trapped into the individualism characteristic of post-Enlightenment ethics. Christian ethics is inherently communitarian, as Paul Lehmann and many others have constantly insisted. It has koinonia at its heart. This is well expressed in the material from Newbigin and Niles with which this paper started, and in Hauerwas's constant reiteration that the church does not have, but is a social ethic, that the church is called to be a criteriological institution, to act as a paradigmatic community. One cannot be a Christian in isolation, only in relationship. Christian ethics is accordingly always *church ethics*. It inevitably confronts the individualist assumptions of modern thought and modern practice, with a stress on the necessity of community and an understanding of human beings as persons-in-relation. It is therefore necessarily communitarian. But Christian ethics is not the in-house discourse of an enclosed community leading a ghetto-like existence, without accepting responsibility for the "world". It makes universal claims about the good as such, not simply about the good that happens to be chosen by Christians. Christian understandings of forgiveness, reconciliation and justice, as we are seeing, even as I write, in the work of the Truth and Reconciliation commission in South Africa, have urgent relevance to the public realm.

Just as Christian ecclesial ethics is opposed to individualism, so it cannot accept a free-floating communitarianism or regard collectivist ethics resting on socialist or other understandings of community as adequate. The church gives a special shape to the understanding of community, a shape which has become specially relevant in an age when on the one hand there is much fragmentation and breakdown of community, and on the other hand still powerful forms of collectivism which diminish human beings and human freedom through a coercive uniformity. The challenge of today is to rediscover what it is to be the church of Jesus Christ for the sake of the world. And this is a costly quest.

Newbigin and Niles are right to stress the primary significance of church as *congregation*. This is the basic and most visible ecclesial reality. Within the local community the people witness to the truth of the gospel on which they are nurtured, and strive to live by grace. The congregation is called to be the body of Christ in that place, to show the love and the justice of God by living faithful lives. Others see, or fail to see, the Lord through the prism of the congregation, and the congregation is summoned to faithfulness. The way the congregation deploys its resources, maintains its buildings, deals with its disputes, develops loving relationships, relates to offenders, and shows itself to be serious about truth and goodness are almost sacramental signs of the truth by which it lives. In a real sense they confirm or question that truth.

But the church is also *national church*, or *volkskirche*, ministering to the national community, confronting that community, whether it is strong and cohesive or fragmented and bitterly divided, with the gospel. A national church is in special danger of assimilating to the ethos of the broader community, embracing its standards, and sacralizing its authority structures — as we have been reminded again and again by the history of the 20th century. But a national church has an important sociological characteristic which the congregation rarely has, and other social organizations hardly ever: it incorporates within the one fellowship people from radically different sectors of society

and at its best enables honest and direct communication and fellowship between the rich and the poor, the learned and those with learning
difficulties, the aristocracy and the underclass. The congregation
tends to be composed of people who are rather like one another, who
come from the same neighbourhood; the national church is more likely
to include a kind of cross-section of the nation. In the past, under the
principle *cuius regio eius religio* it was often assumed that everyone
within a nation or state belonged or should belong to the same church
(e.g. Hooker). Although many Christians who should know better are
nostalgic for that past condition, it is beyond the horizon of possibility
today, and was always ecclesiologically suspect. But the notion that
the national church has a responsibility for the whole life of the nation,
and should in its own life show how divisions and enmities in the life
of the nation may be healed, and have been healed, is of continuing
relevance.

My favourite example of this comes from a troubled part of my
own country — Northern Ireland. Enda McDonagh, the Irish theologian, reminds us that baptism as incorporation into the dying and
rising of Christ is baptism into the one church, which is the body of
Christ. This is not a purely legal point — that different denominations
accept the validity of baptismal initiation into membership — but goes
far deeper. Nor is it simply a reminder that a national church must be a
manifestation of the *una sancta* rather than an expression of civil
religion and nothing more. In our division, or rather, despite our
divisions, we all share in Christ. The celebration of a baptism
involves, he argues, not only the congregation, denomination or
confession, the national church or ethnic Christian fellowship in
which it takes place, but all the other Christian communities. Only so
is it capable of signifying credibly the true nature of the church, the
coming unity of all humankind, and a gospel which has the power to
overcome ancient antagonisms. The poet John Donne wrote in his
early-17th century English:

> The Church is Catholike, universal, so are all her Actions; All that she
> does, belongs to all. When she baptizes a child, that action concerns mee;
> for that child is thereby connected to that Head which is my Head too, and
> engraffed into that body, whereof I am a member... All [hu]mankinde is
> of one Author, and is one volume... [12]

McDonagh develops his theme of the costly, disturbing unity expressed in baptism:

In the more confined world of Northern Ireland, with its overspill in Scotland, England and the Republic of Ireland, this understanding of baptism presents a particular challenge. When asked what the churches could do to help overcome the divisions in Northern Ireland, I sometimes, as a shock tactic, reply: "They should stop baptizing." After the inevitable shock effect I go on to explain how the theological and ecclesiological significance of baptism may be undermined by its social and political significance. Baptism of a new member into the local Church of Ireland or Presbyterian Church or Catholic Church has the same profound theological and ecclesiological significance. It is baptism into the one Christ, the one great Church. All the churches are called to recognize this... However, at this level of history and politics, of peoples' attitudes and divisions, the unity in Christ, the surrender to Christ, is obscured, if not rendered entirely futile. Baptism into a particular church, Protestant or Catholic, expresses integration into a particular historical community of Christians with its own cultural and political traditions which set it apart from and indeed against another community of Christians... To preserve the sacraments from such futility should one not stop the practice of baptism?[13]

McDonagh's suggestion arises out of a passion that the authentic meaning and significance of baptism should shine forth, and an awareness that distortion often enters in, precisely because the true notion of the one church present in the nation to exemplify the reconciliation that has been achieved in Christ has been replaced by a variety of "churches", each in practice representing and defending the interests of one section of the nation.

The church is also actualized in that ecclesiologically strange modern phenomenon, the *denomination*, and the broader manifestation of denominationalism, the confessional family. I cannot here explore the deep ambiguities and problems that surround the idea of the church as denomination, or the shadow side of the development of confessional families in recent decades. I want just to make one simple but important point: in a denomination or confessional family a variety of ethnic groups, cultures and rich and poor come together from various nations. A denomination (like other manifestations of church) has its own power structure, and its own resources, human and material. How it deals with these things indicates how seriously it takes the gospel as the basis for its ecclesial existence, and how effectively it may be able to witness to secular organizations which have structural similarities — corporations, trade unions, NGOs, for example.

The ecumenical community: ethical implications

The "church" which is emerging out of the ecumenical movement, that "great new fact of the 20th century", presents an increasingly well-established ecclesial reality which has clear ethical implications. The oikoumene is already a reality, which influences behaviour and the way we all understand what it is to be church. There is a quite new sense of accountability to one another within the oikoumene. The ecumenical movement has become not just a forum for moral and doctrinal discourse, but a normative model of "church", which challenges more narrow understandings.

Let me give one example of how this works. After the Falklands/ Malvinas War, Margaret Thatcher's government in the UK wanted a victory service of thanksgiving in St Paul's cathedral, London. Unlike earlier occasions of a similar sort, this time from the beginning it was assumed that the major Christian churches should be involved, not just the established Church of England. In the planning of the service it quickly became clear that many of the church leaders would refuse to take part in a triumphalistic service which did not recognize the ambiguity of the conflict and the depth of suffering, anger and confusion that remained in its wake. The church leaders were aware in a new way that what was said and done in St Paul's cathedral would be noted around the world, including in Argentina. They felt themselves to be accountable in a real sense to the oikoumene, and accordingly they arranged a service which, to the fury of government leaders, was chastened and penitent. They were determined that the service should be an act of the Christian church rather than a ritual of civil religion.

At all these levels, the *una sancta* is manifested in its rich diversity and unity. The church, we are reminded, is a global reality, embracing a complex tradition, present in countless lands and cultures and encompassing in the *communio sanctorum* both the dead and generations yet unborn. Both the oneness of the church and the holiness of the church have profound ethical implications. The oneness is the calling of the church to manifest in its life the victory of Christ over hostility, division and violence; the holiness of the church is its calling to demonstrate the capacity of gospel holiness to transform or subvert conventional accounts of goodness, right and justice. The *una sancta* in its common life redefines goodness and provides — or ought to provide — a different, truer and more fulfilling understanding of community.

The churches' ethical and prophetic engagement with society insistently raises the question of church unity, and doctrinal agreements and convergences among churches demand ethical expression. Yet ethical differences between and within churches, on issues as various as abortion or apartheid, can threaten the unity of the church. But as we have seen in recent times in relation to apartheid such divisions, correctly handled, can be the way to a profounder sense of what it is to be the *una sancta*, an experience of the *costliness* of unity.

I find Alasdair MacIntyre's analysis of the modern predicament as breakdown of community and ethical fragmentation compellingly attractive. MacIntyre discerns a massive crisis of community and of morality in the modern world, so that we are in a new Dark Ages, whether we recognize it as such or not. In the famous conclusion to *After Virtue* he draws a comparison with the old Dark Ages, when men and women of intelligence, faith and good will ceased to identify the continuance of civility and moral community with the propping up of the Roman imperium. Instead, they explored the tradition and established communities of shared faith in which they could "live in truth" and offer an alternative understanding of life and of community and of morality. He goes on to suggest that modern morality is only fragments wrested from a tradition which has been rejected or forgotten. It lacks coherence, and fails to attract the degree of support it needs if it is to provide a basis for healthy community life together.

My feeling is that if there is anything to be said for MacIntyre's diagnosis, the Christian response should be twofold: on the one hand, commending Christian ethical "fragments" in the hope that some of them may be recognized as public truth, and that then people may enquire as to the quarry from which they came. This is, in a way, ethical evangelism, or at least a recognition that law and gospel cannot be separated. On the other hand, it is essential that the church, like MacIntyre's communities of shared faith, should present a kind of working model of community and of virtue, the gospel manifested in the life of a community, the church. Modern secular ethics claims to be independent both of theology and of metaphysics. Commonly now it seeks a fragile grounding in consensus. We face a new situation, which is also a new opportunity. And we can only grasp that opportunity with the church in its varied manifestations providing a hermeneutic for law and gospel.

In the fragmented and confusing post-modern world, as in the Sri Lankan or Indian village, the church as the people of God stands not so much at the centre of things, in the middle, as at the margins. But there it is still a visible invitation to all in as far as it strives to live by grace and hope and forgiveness. It witnesses to the gospel and interprets the gospel by living by the gospel. The church is called to live in truth, to abide in truth, to dwell in truth — a Christian notion developed in recent times with fascinating relevance and urgency by thinkers as different as the scientist philosopher Michael Polanyi and by the dissident-turned-statesman Vaclav Havel. Living in truth is not, and cannot be, an individual affair. It involves solidarity. The community that lives in truth cannot be introverted, partial, *incurvatus in se* (turned in on itself). There must be an element of universality and openness to it. This community, according to Havel,

> must foreshadow a general salvation and, thus, it is not just the expression of an introverted, self-contained responsibility that individuals have to and for themselves alone, but responsibility to and for the world. [14]

It is a kind of counter-culture, an alternative which anticipates the future and nourishes hope. But it is not a ghetto; the very notion of living in truth is inescapably open to the neighbour and the neighbour's needs. The community is responsible for the world and for those who do not belong to the community of faith. God has given it specific responsibilities and opportunities in the place and time in which God has placed it. Its obedience is "costly" if it indeed dissents from dominant themes in the society in which it is set, and offers a different model, the koinonia of dwelling together in truth.

In a very different way, Polanyi, scientist, philosopher and Christian thinker, sees the Christian mode of dwelling in truth and conviviality as something that cannot be *enjoyed*, precisely because the truth and goodness in which one dwells is not something one may possess or be at ease in. It is a way of life which is challenging, risky, costly, disturbing. The truth is always call as well as gift:

> The confession of guilt, the surrender to God's mercy, the prayer for grace, the praise of God, bring about mounting tension. By the ritual acts the worshipper accepts the obligation to achieve what he knows to be beyond his own unaided powers and strives towards it in the hope of a merciful visitation from above. The ritual of worship is expressly designed to induce and sustain this state of anguish, surrender and hope. The moment a man were to claim that he had arrived and could now happily contemplate his own perfection, he would be thrown back into spiritual emptiness. [15]

The church as a pilgrim people is committed to a truth and a goodness that it knows to be both beyond its grasp and constantly offered as pure gift. It is sustained by the gospel in its dwelling in and journeying towards truth and love.

The community that lives by the gospel also delights in the law. And the world needs both gospel and law. In that order.

NOTES

[1] See his address to the Uppsala assembly on "The Mandate of the Ecumenical Movement", 4 July 1968, in *The Uppsala Report 1968*, Norman Goodall, ed., Geneva, WCC, 1968, pp.313ff. (here p.320).

[2] See p.6 of this volume, para. 7.6.

[3] See p.30 of this volume, para. 22.

[4] "Report of Section IV", in *On the Way to Fuller Koinonia: Official Report of the Fifth World Conference on Faith and Order*, Thomas F. Best and Günther Gassmann, eds, Faith and Order paper no. 166, Geneva, WCC, 1994, para. 25, p.259.

[5] *Truth to Tell: The Gospel as Public Truth*. London, SPCK, 1991, p.35.

[6] *Upon the Earth: The Mission of God and the Missionary Enterprise of the Churches*, Madras, Christian Literature Society, 1962, p.197.

[7] *Honest Religion for Secular Man*, London, SCM, 1966, p.108.

[8] *Ibid.*

[9] *Truthfulness and Tragedy*, Notre Dame, Notre Dame UP, 1977, pp.142-43, emphasis added.

[10] Television interview with Melvyn Bragg, Channel 4, England, March 1994.

[11] *The Human Condition*, New York, Doubleday Anchor Books, 1959, p.215.

[12] *Devotions*, XVII.

[13] *Between Chaos and New Creation*, Dublin, Gill & Macmillan, 1986, pp.84-85.

[14] *Living in Truth*, London, Faber, 1987, p.103.

[15] *Personal Knowledge*, London, Routledge, 1958, p.198.

The Right Direction,
but a Longer Journey

LARRY RASMUSSEN

"In the church's own struggles for justice, peace, and the integrity of creation, the *esse* of the church is at stake."[1] "Costly Obedience" develops the potential of "moral formation", suggested at Tantur, as a promising way to articulate this core assertion about being church. Much is thereby gained. Moral formation *is* a fruitful basis for work together across the rich mix of ecclesiologies present in the WCC. But then "Costly Obedience" brings to premature closure its own best suggestion for discovering the concrete moral dimensions of ecclesiology. Such at least is the contention of this reflection.

"Can a distinctive, shared ecumenical formation come to exist under specific local circumstances? Can it come to exist globally?"[2] These questions go to the heart of "Costly Obedience". They carry forward the line of challenges so ably put in "Costly Commitment":

> Is it enough to say (as we did in *Church and World* and *Costly Unity*) that ethical engagement is intrinsic to the church *as* church? Is it enough to say that, if a church is not engaging responsibly with the ethical issues of its day, it is not being fully church? Must we not also say: if the churches are not engaging these ethical issues *together,* then *none of them individually is being fully church*?[3]

The form here is consciously rhetorical. It means to say that individual churches are not fully church if theirs is not an ecumenical quest for justice, peace and creation's integrity.

"Costly Obedience" answers this line of inquiry about the church's nature by pushing the "how" question to the fore. ("Can a distinctive, shared ecumenical formation come to exist...?") It asks whether a process exists, or might come to be, that lets ecumenical relationships among the various churches assist the cause of each in forming its members in the gospel. More precisely, it asks whether there is a way to effect moral formation in a manner appropriate to each church's moral witness in its specific locale, as that moral witness expresses the way of life implicit in each church's self-understanding as church. The suggestiveness of such questions is the gift of "Costly Obedience", as successor to "Costly Unity" and "Costly Commitment".

Yet this very suggestiveness would be simply formal in nature, and hollow, apart from "Costly Obedience"'s rich exploration of moral formation. Only careful reading, study and discussion for each church's life, and the churches together, can do justice to this, the heart of the report. A summary cannot. Nonetheless, some notes are necessary, for the sake of the proposed process itself.

A new approach to moral formation

"Costly Obedience" recalls the prior consultations' claim that the church not only *has*, but *is*, a social ethic. The church will form — or malform — those whose lives are shaped by liturgy, cathechesis, moral witness, church order, or any other expression in its life. Its very structure and the manner in which its members relate to one another and the wider society constitute a social ethic. Moral formation — and malformation — is inevitable as an expression of the lived life and shape of churches. "Costly Obedience" wants to do nothing so much as make this entire, inevitable process self-conscious, for the specific purpose of "an intentional mutual upbuilding". [4]

Inescapable pluralism reigns here. Churches create, modify and draw deeply from differing traditions. They face different moral challenges. Understandings, emphases and expressions of moral formation differ accordingly. The sense of moral identity, the ordering of community, the pattern of motivation, the place and meaning given specific rites and practices will, even amidst strong continuities, vary from church to church and locale to locale as compelling needs and issues arise and evolve.

One conclusion of "Costly Obedience" is that all formation is irreducibly concrete and local. It happens person-by-person in congregations and parishes. Congregations engender certain ways of seeing life "just by being the kinds of communities they are". Ecclesiastical polities "play out in certain forms of life, certain ways of living, which shape the way church members comport themselves in the world". [5] The process is full of detail and anything but abstract. This realization drives another. The attention must go to "the specific way" communities of faith form their members. We must ask "about the actual thinking that goes on in these worshipping communities".[6] Focus on formation means investigation of "actual communities with their cultures" and "the complex 'thickness' of lives actually lived".[7] "There is [thus] no way of talking about 'Christian ethics' without asking how the congregation [actually] functions in moral formation."[8]

"Costly Obedience" has taken a certain quiet, crucial turn here. It suggests, in effect, that linkages of ecclesiology and ethics are not effectively answered *at the normative level alone*. Assertions of what "the church" *is*, normatively (the "marks" of the church), when pursued apart from "actual communities with their cultures" and "the actual thinking that goes on in... worshipping communities" will not move the ecumenical agenda of visible unity forward. It will not discover the fruitfulness, or even the form, of moral formation as an ecumenical enterprise. Rather, the way forward is a process or processes by which churches "articulate their own particular ways of acting out the story of Jesus in the world"[9] in all its concreteness, in the presence of one another. This may indeed lead to discovering common marks of the church — catholicity, for example, or the imperative for justice. Unity itself may be discovered by such means. If so, it will be discovered, or realized, in the churches' "actual communities with their cultures",[10] and in ways we can see, feel, taste and touch, rather than settled by normative theological claims about the nature of the church as given.

Differently said, the most promising way forward is not that of finding the language of normative common ground as that might be offered by theologians and agreed to by heads of communions. This understanding of ecumenical formation is essentially doctrinal and jurisdictional. The most promising way is arranging a common table, open to participation by the whole people of God, to see what emerges as living church when faith is freely shared on the burning issues we face. Ecumenical formation here is more inductive than deductive, the outcome of a shared experience of engaged church. Here ecumenical moral formation happens by way of testimony to the moral life as the life of faith as churches face their own pressing issues, opportunities and problems.

Moral formation as shared experience

The "Theology of Life" conference near Nairobi, 13-19 January 1997, was a sample of common table methodology done ecumenically. The form was "Sokoni", the African market-place for exchanges of all kinds — goods, information, ideas, networks and plans, stories, music, gossip and deliberation. Church groups of all kinds came from throughout Kenya to express in ways they chose — drama, music, study, testimony, conversation, dance — what "being church" meant in their "actual lived communities with their cultures". These churches joined commissioned case studies on issues of justice, peace and creation as reported from 23 countries around the world — a microcosm of the world church. The format of reporting these studies also varied, as chosen by those most deeply involved (the case study coordinators were present). To this was added the salient results of the team visits of the Ecumenical Decade of the Churches in Solidarity with Women, the work and issues of youth, the contributions of indigenous peoples, and continuing struggles against racism, poverty and violence. While utterly engaging, Sokoni was not a kind of ecumenical floor show and exhibit hall. It was "market" as community common table and a way of conducting business together. Individual churches and scattered peoples who often do not collaborate ecumenically found themselves rubbing shoulders in shared story, witness and deliberation.

Granted, "Sokoni" did not go far enough. We needed more time to pursue the ecclesial experience we shared, to explore its implications and its contradictions. We needed opportunity to continue the joint moral formation here set on its way. But doing that does not mean adding another method to this style of ecumenical work. It means continuing this very method and its logic, a logic that thrives *on multiple points of entry* in witnessing to the life of faith, *as expressed through varied media by the whole people of God* — young and old, lettered and unlettered, male and female, of whatever race, clan, nationality and ecclesial tradition. The road that uses selected representatives of a certain stratum to work together in consultations near some airport so as to produce documents and resolutions which are then commended to the WCC and its member churches in the hope of common action, is not the road taken here. Here the effort is a rich ecumenical mix, locally and regionally, as that is planned, effected and owned by participants, with the kind of help the WCC, as a global body, can offer (networks, experience, financial and other resources, and complementary staff).

"Costly Obedience" goes a long way in this promising direction. It almost writes the development of such a method as the way to answer its own lead question of how ecumenical moral formation can be effected locally and globally simultaneously. It celebrates the "freedom to seek new patterns" and the search to "transcend old vocabularies". It wants to focus on "the immediate and local" and suggests "resonance and recognition" as criteria across differences (see part IV, "Towards Communion in Moral Witnessing"). Furthermore, it knows some of the traps: "It is important not to drain the fullness from our language by defining our terms purely conceptually, juridically or ecclesiastically, and not also morally. Nor must we let some particular structural aspect of the church's life be considered the sole fulfillment of what this language means." [11]

Discovering the unity of the church

But in the end it forecloses on its own process. It is still preoccupied, as the foregoing sentence indicates, with "language". Its bias is finding common ecumenical "discourse" and "voice", not as the outcome of ecumenical process but as initial common ground. Likewise it searches, in an explication of the sacraments, for shared "moral communion". Since mutual recognition of eucharist is still an ecumenical sticking point, its turn is to baptism as the source of common moral content across churches. "There is enough moral substance lodged in the reality of our common baptism to justify some sort of ecumencial space-making right now for that shared spiritual gift." [12]

But this subtlely, probably unwittingly, subverts the very promise offered. The bias towards finding common discourse and shared substance in the sacraments will sideline a more basic, and more promising, effort. It will likely end up reinserting the need to agree upon theologically normative categories and criteria. The norms, then, do not emerge from what is discovered together; they become the stipulation of participation itself. "Costly Obedience" has it exactly right when it asks, "How do we make room on earth for this oikoumene of mutually recognized resonance among our ways of concrete moral-ecclesial being-in-the-world?" [13] And it has it exactly right when it describes the WCC's task as "marker and space-maker for an ecumenical moral communion". But it crimps the process, rather than effecting it, when it tries to anticipate what we should find. For the next period, we should not try to do more than create a space "where language is constantly sought to express the reality more fully, where common actions are conceived which embody the needed moral witness, and where an ecumenical formation takes place which gives growing density, increasing fullness, to it".[14] (Concretely, this means, to cite one instance, exploring and developing the method expressed in the Theology of Life Programme, the team visits of the Ecumenical Decade of the Churches in Solidarity with Women, and the Programme to Overcome Violence's "Peace to the Cities" campaign.)

In the end, the "costly" of "Costly Unity", "Costly Commitment" and "Costly Obedience" has a meaning we did not anticipate when the study process and the three consultations were planned. We were well aware of the initial, important meaning; namely, the price paid "in pursuing justice and peace";[15] the price paid, in different words, in taking up, as a matter of faith, morally contested issues that might disturb the "unity" of the church. Now we learn of another cost as well. It is the cost of arranging a process that risks the *discovery* of the visible unity of the church in open-ended exchange, rather than asserting it normatively as a condition of sincere participation. The cost is that of a common table open to high levels of participation by all, rather than stipulating agreed-upon common ground as a prerequisite for entering ecumenical space.

This kind of space for grace and the unpredictable ways of the Holy Spirit in a time when norms themselves are everywhere contested could well be costly for all. And life-giving! But in a period "when the earth seems to shake from the forces of change, and there is no way to foresee what specific forms an authentic Christian way of life will take in coming years",[16] a time "altogether determined by things that are no longer and things that are not yet",[17] just such a risk seems the way forward together.

NOTES

[1] "Costly Commitment", see p.47 of this volume, para. 71, echoing "Costly Unity", para. 5 (p.4).
[2] Para. 34.
[3] Para. 17c, emphasis original.
[4] Para. 35.
[5] Para. 20.
[6] Para. 20.
[7] Para. 17.
[8] Para. 20.
[9] Para. 61.

[10] Para. 17.
[11] Para. 97.
[12] Para. 104.
[13] Para. 98.
[14] Para. 102.
[15] "Costly Unity", para. 7.6.
[16] *Practising our Faith: A Way of Life for a Searching People*, Dorothy Bass, ed., San Francisco, Jossey-Bass, 1997, p.203.
[17] Hannah Arendt, as cited by Gar Alperowitz in "The Reconstruction of Community Meaning", *Tikkun*, vol. 11, no. 3, p.79.

Reflections of a Filipina Christian

ELIZABETH S. TAPIA

What happens when the church is silent? What happens when the church is active? What happens when the church is prophetic? What happens when the church is anaemic? What happens when the church is oppressive and insensitive to marginalized groups such as women, youth, the differently-abled, sexual and political outcasts, the unchurched?

Why does the church exist? For whom and with whom does it exist? How does the church function in a culture of violence, greed and exploitation? What to do with myriads of mammon? Is the "doing" of the church congruent with its "being"? These are questions I have been reflecting on since I began to participate in the study process on ecclesiology and ethics.

The "who and the what" of the church is best understood by its "why": its reason for living, its mission and witness. Conversely, its mission and witness are shaped by its theology and self-understanding.

Portrait of a church

What makes the church church? Is it the people? Is it the Spirit of the Lord Jesus Christ? Is it the context or situation the church finds itself in? Is it the collective commitment and worship of the believers of Christ? Is it all of the above?

A church that refuses to listen to the voices of women, who comprise more than half of its members, is one that is irrelevant and exclusive. A church that participates in the discrimination and exploitation of women, men and children is a sick one; while a church that takes seriously and gratefully the gifts and participation of women is one that is destined to grow. A church where harmony, mutual understanding and equality exist is a dynamic and healthy community.

A church that learns from the wisdom of the indigenous peoples and recognizes the strength of the old is one that is vibrant, creative and contagious.

A church that condones violence and sexual abuse is contributing to the perpetuation of human degradation.

"Where was the church when we were imprisoned?" asked a young woman at the height of the martial law dictatorship under the Marcos regime. "Are the churches tired of helping us?" groaned an old man who lost his entire family, house and farmland to the rampage of mudflow brought down by the Mt Pinatubo eruption. "Why does my church refuse to ordain women?" A young Asian feminist replied: "Your church does not want to ordain women because it is afraid of women and what they can do."

A church that overflows with "shoulds and musts" and lacks a spirit of openness can easily become dogmatic, legalistic and boring. A church that celebrates life in the midst of struggles and forces of death knows the value of every moment and the sacredness of every life.

To be involved is to die, and to die is to live again

On 4 February 1997 the well-loved Roman Catholic bishop Benjamin de Jesus was murdered in front of the cathedral in Jolo, Sulu, Mindanao. The Philippine daily newspapers carried this tragic news on the front pages for two weeks. Bishop de Jesus, who belonged to the Oblate fathers, was loved and respected by both Muslims and Christians in Mindanao for his commitment and work for justice, peace and reconciliation in war-torn areas.

Because he embodied a reconciling love between Muslims and Christians, he was called a "Christian Imam". Because he practised what he preached, Bishop Benjamin de Jesus influenced the moral character of his parishioners. He passionately pursued the radical teaching of Jesus to walk the second mile when needed; to love, not to hate; to share, not to hoard; to serve, not to be served. He ate, walked, worshipped, laughed, worked with Christians and Muslims for many years.

But Bishop de Jesus' life was cut short by seven deadly bullets fired allegedly by an extremist Muslim father and son. The wake, which lasted ten days and nights, was attended by the poor and the rich, government officials and church officials, women and men, children and old, Muslims and Christians. He was buried on 15 February and on that day the life, faith and service of this church leader were etched forever on the hearts of the Filippino people. It was a costly reconciliation.

In many third-world countries people do not have the luxury to sit down for a week to define the "being of the church". They become the living church in the everyday struggle for food, shelter, jobs, water, and so on. Like the early church, they worship and eat together; they share their resources, however meagre, with those in need. Liturgies and protests in picket lines, poetry, drama and dances expressing people's theologies, boycotting Nestlé products, confidence-building in peace talks, Bible studies under the mango trees, praying with the sick, marching in protest against the violence and abuse of women at home and in media — all these speak of the ethical reflection and theological conviction of the church.

An assessment of the study process on ecclesiology and ethics

1. The study process gave opportunities to discern, correct and redirect the perceived tension between the doctrinal and social justice concerns of the WCC.

2. The study process was able to point up clearly the basic affirmation that ecclesiology and ethics can and should relate with each other. At the Tantur consultation, we realized that "the quest for unity and the struggle for justice are integral to the life of the church".

3. If one of the striking qualities of "Costly Unity" is its sense of urgency, as pointed out by William Henn, then "Costly Commitment" calls us to a process of discernment and involvement of the church as a moral community in the world today. The Tantur report considers Christ's believers as called together in a constant process of discernment "how best to participate, in the light of our faith, in the moral struggles, complexities and challenges facing humankind".

4. In my opinion, such a constant process of discernment can be influenced by our moral and ethical decisions and moral formation, as well as our theological and doctrinal beliefs.

I found the discussion on Christian moral formation very helpful, but it also made me reflect on the reality of various types of moral formation. Christians do not have the monopoly on moral formation. Consequently, we need to learn from other faith traditions. What is unique in their beliefs? How does their faith stance influence the way they live and the way they die?

5. We need to engage in a critical self-understanding of the church. We must review how our doctrinal and ethical teachings either help or hinder, negate or promote the full humanity of women, the empowerment of the laity and the respectful relating with other religious faiths and communities.

6. The study process brought together theologians and ethicists from all over the world to reflect together and critique each other's stances. There is a need to pursue this on a small-scale, at the grassroots level, not only with those who are academically trained and ecumenically exposed, but even more with grassroots theologians, wise folk in villages, elders in indigenous communities, mothers, activist groups, feminist groups, NGO leaders, etc.

7. What I found lacking in the study process was a consistent critique of power relations between church and state, between women and men, the haves and the have-nots. Also the equal representation of women and men needs rethinking. The majority of voices heard were men's. Was the study process on ecclesiology and ethics purely academic? How can it touch the lives and concerns of people at the grassroots? In what manner do we speak? What language do we use? How do we listen and discern? How can the results of this talk be made available to people and groups like those mentioned in point 6 above?

I found exciting the case study shared by John de Gruchy on South Africa's post-apartheid commission on Truth and Reconciliation. Chaired by Archbishop Desmond Tutu, this commission is a visible expression of how the church and the government can work together, in the light of their faith and commitment, for justice, truth-telling and justice-making. I admired the courage and *costly commitment* of the people of South Africa as they struggled against the oppressive system of apartheid. While we were meeting in Johannesburg, we had a chance to worship in a black Anglican church in Soweto. We were hosted at an ecumenical dinner by Brigalia Bam, the general secretary of the South African Council of Churches, where we shared in the aspirations and dreams of South African church leaders as they work for the reconstruction of their country.

8. In Tantur, we talked about the eucharist, but we did not share in the Lord's table because even in our small elite group of theologians and ethicists we were not able to transcend our theological dif-

ferences. How sad that was for me. We worshipped together, we shared meals and ideas together; but even while reflecting on the "costly commitment" we could not share in the eucharist.

9. I feel that many of our churches still have a dualistic view of church and society, theology and ethics, faith and witness, doctrine and deed, matter and spirit. How we move beyond dualism and absolutism is another task.

Future tasks, directions and vision

• To continue working towards the visible unity among churches by promoting visible inclusiveness in the churches (at local, district, national and regional levels). Churches need to be conscious of whom they are excluding from their life and witness and how they can become more inclusive so everyone has a place and a voice.

• To explore intergenerational, interdisciplinary, intercultural, intergender approaches to ethical issues like economic injustice, reproductive rights, conflict management, technological cloning, effects of globalization, ecological crises, bio-medical ethics and others.

• To generate genuine, lasting ecumenism at all levels (local, national, global) and in all areas (liturgical, political, ethical and so on).

• To include and learn from the feminist ecclesiology and feminist ethics. The dominant traditional ecclesiology reinforces the subjugation of women and the domination of men. So often church mission is viewed only as the salvation of the soul, never mind the body. Traditional patriarchal ethics do not take the experiences and the wellbeing of women seriously. For example, ethical rules for women are most often made by men.

• To deal with issues of violence. The report of the team visits related to the Ecumenical Decade of Churches in Solidarity with Women reveals an alarming problem of violence against women in Christian homes and churches. The church cannot remain a church when more than half of its people are abused, violated, humiliated or disenfranchised. Our ecclesiology must necessarily be pro-women.

• To promote a liberating kind of religious education in homes, schools, seminaries, churches, mosques, playground and elsewhere.

• To practise the full participation of youth, women and lay people whenever church doctrines and ethical teachings are formulated and enforced.

• To deal with issues of powers. What must the church do when one of its members or leaders is silenced or excommunicated, as in the case of Tissa Balasuriya of Sri Lanka?

• To deal with issues of exclusion. Women everywhere suffer from sexism, classism and racism. Are the churches in solidarity with women? Are churches a safe place for women? How can women and men experience genuine partnership in church and society?

• To develop and articulate an integral spirituality that embodies an interconnectedness of faith and action, prayer and protest, doctrines and deeds, visible unity among believers of Christ, visible compassion and justice towards the exploited and oppressed, confession and celebration, unity and commitment.

Closing remarks

I have no ready answers to the questions posed at the beginning of this reflection. I hear them so many times and they remain in my heart to ponder. But I know I must do something to make my being part of the church relevant.

In a third-world country like the Philippines, we have a smorgasbord of crises: economic, ecological, relational, moral and health. There are so many threats to life; survival is the name of the game. The greatest challenge confronting the church in the Philippines today is how to discern and embody a vision of shalom, peace with justice, a vision of healing and wholeness for all peoples and creation.

Churches and theological seminaries need to look at realities from the perspective of the poor and their faith struggles, their powerlessness, their spirituality, their oppression and also their willingness to die for the sake of friends, loved ones and motherland.

Fortunately, there are movements in my country and around the world that help give birth to change: the human rights movement, the indigenous people's movement, the peace movement, the ecology movement and the women's movement. The church can be a movement of women and men committed to preach and actualize the gospel in ways that will generate peace, justice, harmony, healing and wholeness. People in these movements must work together to bring total transformation in church and society.

I sincerely hope that the study process on ecclesiology and ethics will not end with its funding and programmatic deadlines, but will be pursued, with the guidance of the Holy Spirit, with a growing sense of unity and deeper commitment even to the point of *costly reconciliation*.

Thoughts on the Study on "Ecclesiology and Ethics"

1. The question of the relationship between ecclesiology and ethics belongs with that of koinonia and JPIC, and also of church and world. Such questions point not only to an as-yet-unresolved tension which surfaces regularly within the WCC, but also to the WCC's sometimes controversial approach to the world, or at any rate to various political, social or economic circumstances in the world. The churches in the WCC do not yet seem to have achieved clarity or agreement on the tension between the understanding of the church and the churches' practical commitment in the world.

The fact that ecclesiology and ethics, or the understanding of the church and the churches' practical action, belong together seems to be generally accepted within the WCC. In other words, there is no need for further demonstration that ecclesiology and ethics belong together. Further work and in-depth reflection are, however, needed on *how* ecclesiology and ethics relate to one another within the WCC and beyond it, and on how the churches together within the WCC relate to the world — not least to accompany the current discussion on the paper on "A Common Understanding and Vision of the WCC".

In the first instance, this has to do with the fundamental question of the aims of the WCC. Most of the criticism which has led us back again and again to the problem of ecclesiology and ethics seems definitely to stem from unclarity as to whether the WCC really is the structure for the restoration of unity among the churches, or whether it is simply an instrument for common practical action by the churches. Whether and how far the WCC also exists as a structure for *Christians* may be left open for the moment.

The question here is not so much whether the WCC has successfully integrated the two great streams of Life and Work and Faith and

Order, not to mention mission and evangelism, but perhaps more directly how the Council now understands its aims. Is it both a structure serving the restoration of church unity and an instrument for common practical action by the churches? Was not the reason for bringing Life and Work and Faith and Order together precisely in order to help the churches rediscover and restore their visible unity? If this is so, then it should still be assumed that the more the churches take common action on practical issues, the closer they will draw to their visible unity; and conversely, the deeper the churches' agreement on their respective ecclesiologies, the more they will act together on practical issues.

2. The tension between ecclesiology and ethics apparently lies more in the fear of one-sidedness. Those who see ecclesiology as fundamental in the discussion on the way to visible unity — here one may mention the view of Orthodox churches as an example — fear that the WCC is too concerned with practical issues, to the detriment of the quest for unity. On the other side are those who say that the WCC's credibility depends not on its sometimes very theoretical theological discourse, but on its commitment to practical action in and for the world. Are we dealing here with different expectations or does this tension go deeper? Is it not itself "ecclesiological" in character? Is it not that for some Christians "what the church is and means" (ecclesiology) is more important, while for others it is "how the church appears and acts" (ethics)?

In the modern world, ethics can easily exist without ecclesiology, but not the reverse. That is to say, an ethics based on ecclesiology has a special character; it differs from general ethics. In this case, what kind of ecclesiology and above all what kind of ethics are we talking about?

The recent study on ecclesiology and ethics[1] has shown how important it is to have coherence in examining these two concerns in the WCC. That is to say, the ethics practised by the WCC should correspond to the ecclesiology it professes. Or, at least, the WCC's ethical commitment must be in harmony with its ecclesiological concern.

In this respect, the WCC should continue the work on ecclesiology in Faith and Order, in close cooperation with the churches. As regards the work of Faith and Order, the question is not whether the latter is doing "classical academic ecumenical theology"[2] or not, but whether its work is helping the churches further along the road to unity. This work should lead on to an ecclesiological vision which can bring the churches closer to one another. Such a vision can only be developed in cooperation with the churches, because a study process of this kind should help the churches to grow together. An ecclesiological vision does not mean that the WCC can develop its own ecclesiology parallel to or separate from the churches. All work on ecclesiology in the WCC, indeed on theological issues in general, needs to be complemented and balanced by work on practical ethical questions.

3. But what of the churches? Is the much-cited "ecumenical winter" a genuine crisis which could undo much that has been done, or is it a "growth crisis" in the history of the ecumenical movement? After their long ecumenical experience the churches should be able to recognize that they have grown together and act accordingly. The member churches of the WCC have formulated and adopted so many common resolutions; held so many lengthy discussions on fundamental theological issues and reached broad consensus or convergence on them; taken a common stance on numerous practical issues; dwelt together in prayer on many occasions. How do the churches perceive this experience? Is this commitment to the ecumenical fellowship not a good basis for further steps?

In practical terms, it may be helpful here to refer to the Lima document. It should be remembered first of all that, leading up to and following on from it, decisive steps forward have been taken by some churches: the Leuenberg Agreement on Church Fellowship (1973), the Meissen Agreement (1988), or Porvoo (1992), to name only a few. A closer look at these different church fellowships shows how important questions of ecclesiology are. Even if these fellowships cannot necessarily be taken as a model for all other churches, the experience is still worth sharing.

To return to the Lima document, it should also be remembered that, together with this text, a Lima *liturgy* was also adopted. What has this liturgy contributed and what does it still signify today? Then again, we should also ask ourselves whether the time is not ripe for the churches to draw the consequences from the fact that baptism in the name of Holy Trinity is recognized by all. Are we, as Christian men and women, bound together by the one baptism over and beyond confessional boundaries, despite the continuing division among our churches? How are we, as still-separate Christians and churches, bound by the tie of our one baptism? On this basis, it should be possible for our churches together to develop an acceptable ecclesiological vision.

4. Commitment for and in the world is part of the nature of the church as a missionary community. True to its original mission, the church is present in the world and for the world, but it is not the world, nor is it identical with it. The church must be engaged in the world through its prophetic service for peace, justice and the integrity of creation, but it does this out of its own conviction and with its own means. And this should never be taken for granted. There are many institutions in the world today much better equipped than the churches to work for peace, justice or reconciliation. The churches should not simply replicate what secular institutions can do better, but should offer a different, deeper dimension for human relations.

The church's motivation for its practical commitment for and in the world springs from its firm belief in the crucified and risen Lord. Conversely, the churches' practical commitment must clearly express the conviction of faith which underlies it. For the church, its practical commitment should be another dimension of its mission for the world, and when this is so its practical commitment will be consistent with its ecclesiology.

Christians and churches are engaged in and for the world because of their faith in the incarnate God, and because in serving their fellow human beings they perhaps draw nearer to God; praying to God and serving humankind are not two quite different things; if all this is done out of love and in faith, then one service runs over into the other. In our modern world full of fears and uncertainty, Christians and the churches must hold more firmly to their faith, that the world may believe and, believing, may rediscover hope and love.

NOTES

[1] See in particular *Ecclesiology and Ethics: Costly Commitment*, Geneva, WCC, 1995.
[2] Peter Lodberg, "The History of Ecumenical Work on Ecclesiology and Ethics", in *ibid.*, p.1.

Contributors

Duncan B. Forrester is professor of Christian ethics and practical theology and dean of the faculty of divinity, University of Edinburgh, Scotland.

Viorel Ionita from Romania is secretary for studies with the Conference of European Churches, Geneva, Switzerland.

Larry Rasmussen is Reinhold Niebuhr professor of social ethics at Union Theological Seminary, New York, and co-moderator of the World Council of Churches' programme unit on justice, peace and creation.

Elizabeth S. Tapia teaches at the Union Theological Seminary of the Philippine Christian Centre of Learning in Dasmarinas (Cavite) and Manila.